Corporate Ladder 101:

How to Excel as a
New Business Professional

Charles A. Lambert

Corona Pass Publishing

Printed in the United States of America

ISBN: 978-0-578-00374-0

This book is dedicated to Luke and Josh who are both a part of the next generation of leaders, movers and shakers ready to climb the corporate ladder. But it is without a doubt dedicated to Jackie who has provided inspiration, belief and encouragement since the first day we met.

Enjoy the climb!

Charlie

Contents

Introduction

There are books that have been written to teach business etiquette. There are books written to show you how to dress for a successful career. There are books for productive presentations, masterful meetings and power-filled sales calls. This book is some of those things and more. It fills the gap that these types of self-help books do not. This book is important to you because it presents you with ideas, tips and advice on how to handle issues and circumstances that may be new to you as you embark on your professional career.

These simple, but effective techniques will help you develop a style that will catapult you through your first year. Not only that, but if you continue to use them throughout your professional life, you will absolutely achieve great success.

The ideas and thoughts presented in this book represent a gathering of experiences not only of my own career, but of other professionals from many different lines of work. Some of these are the result of reflections made when thinking about things like, "What would I have done differently...?" Some of these ideas reflect the things we did that helped us develop good impressions with our supervisors and peers. And some of these ideas are the results of criticisms, advice, reprimands, positive reinforcements, and other observations made by those who felt comfortable in providing such "constructive" suggestions.

What makes the first year in the corporate world so important? What makes it so different than your first year in college, or the first time you got a "real" job when you were in high school?

Well, there are two main reasons why you need to make your first year count. Primarily, you need to immediately begin developing the habits that will set you apart from the pack of peers with whom you will be competing for advancement. Secondarily, but just as important, is that during your first year you will be making impressions that you will be living with for a very long time.

We are all affected by first impressions. You will be making them every day. And with impressions come labels. Once made, they may take years to change. Like a neon light flashing "I Can Do It." Or conversely, like a "Kick Me" sign planted in the middle of your back.

During your first year, you will have labels placed upon you such as "reliable," "independent," "trustworthy," and the like. Your goal now is to have people see your face or hear your name and associate positive, secure images to you. You want people to think of you as a person with whom they would want to do business; somebody they would want on their team. You will accomplish this if you take the suggestions in this book to heart and challenge yourself to put them to use in your daily professional life.

During this first year, you will be constantly evaluated both in and out of the office. People will be sizing you up for many things. It could be for your attitude toward fellow employees and the ability to work as a team. It may be for your reliability and ability to get things done on time, every time. You may be tested for your trustworthiness and your ability to handle confidential information. Your credibility may be put to the test along with your integrity and your ability to follow up on the promises that you make.

People will not only be measuring you up in many ways, but also in many places. Every interaction that you have with a coworker is an opportunity to impress. Of course, you will be making impressions in the workplace, but the playing field is larger than that. It may also be the restaurant during a business luncheon or dinner. You may also be sized up during after-hours social gatherings. This means at the local watering hole during happy hour, in a company carpool, or even at the company softball game.

Your first year is a breeding ground for making impressions and achievements that may last with you for your entire career. It is also a time during which you will be making allies and developing relationships with people that may have a significant impact on your future career path, and ultimately, your destiny in life.

The point is that the things you do today will have an impact on the rest of your life. The good habits you develop today will give you a distinct advantage in your growth and advancement. Some actions that you take will have subtle lasting effects. Some will have monumental effects and may result in the course of your life being changed.

This book will give you a leg up on the corporate ladder by using the collective experiences of those who have already walked this path. Only our walk was alone. You already have an advantage over you peers because you will use the techniques described within these pages that follow to immediately cultivate your professional skills and work habits.

With all this in mind let's have some fun and get to work!

Part I

Hands On

1

And The Award Goes To...

The goal of this book is to equip you with some simple tips, tricks and habits that will help you distinguish yourself from your peers, many of whom may also be new corporate professionals. Face it, these peers may be your friends, but they're also your competitors. You are all on a playing field and the prize is upward mobility; getting off the first rung of the corporate ladder, getting more responsibility, more challenges, more prestige and naturally, more money.

I want you to be set apart, to be thought of as head and shoulders above your workplace competitors, to have everything you need to catapult yourself over those first few rungs of that ladder.

But before we get started, I want you to answer what you may think is a rather bizarre question. You may even think I'm rude to ask you this question. It's a simple "yes" or "no" answer, but I want you to sincerely think through your past as you formulate your response. If you are honest with yourself, the answer you give may be hard to admit and may be hard to take.

So, here is the question: Are you a trophy kid?

For those not familiar with that term, a trophy kid is one most likely born in the 1980s or 1990s. They were most likely very pampered by their parents and as a result have a strong sense of entitlement.

That is, they often feel like someone owes them something just for showing up.

So, what's your answer? Are you a trophy kid?

One way to help think through this is to answer another set of questions. For instance, do you have great expectations…expectations not of yourself, but of others?

More specifically, do you expect your employer to give you flexible hours and mold themselves to your needs and lifestyle? Do you expect to be rewarded by your employer for doing the bare minimum required of your job? Do you believe there are some jobs or tasks that are beneath you, that you'd rather starve to death before doing? Do you expect to be CEO in five years, but don't want to give up your free time? Will you blame someone else if you miss a deadline because you didn't receive a reminder notice?

If after some honest self-evaluation, you come to the conclusion that you may just possibly, on the extreme outside chance of probability, think you're a trophy kid, that's ok. You're not alone. In fact, according to a survey by CareerBuilder.com and as reported in the Wall Street Journal, 85% of hiring managers believe that those born between 1980 – 2001 (a.k.a. The Millennial Generation), "have a much stronger sense of entitlement than do older workers."

Of course being a trophy kid isn't necessarily your own doing – it's the way you were raised. Most parents spoil their kids and want them to have the best of life and avoid hardship. You'll maybe do the same when you become a parent. But you have to admit, after living 20 or so years getting golden trophies even though your soccer team never finished above last place, it may be hard to overcome the expectation that you should be rewarded for just being a participant at your workplace.

Don't get me wrong, I love the trophies. But now that you're in the real world, things just don't work that way. If they did, cops would be pulling you over and giving YOU money just for not breaking the speed limit.

So, maybe you received trophies all your life for just showing up. Maybe that didn't make you feel like you were more special than everyone else. Maybe it did. But at this point, your days of participation trophies are over. As of this moment, if you show up to work, great. Then get to work. If you don't show up, great. You've decided to get yourself fired.

Now, it's all about performance. It's about performance and doing a few extraordinary things. Look at that word "extraordinary." It's a compound word. You can break it down into two words, "extra" and "ordinary." There is a truism in life that states the difference between ordinary performance and extraordinary performance is that little "extra" you put into your effort. Learning how to be extraordinary in your job is what you'll find in the rest of this book.

To be sure, none of the insights described on these remaining pages will be of any use to you if you are not committed to a strong work ethic. As you may already know, life is not always fair, but it is usually a lot more fair to people who work hard and don't sit around waiting for good things to happen to them. Success won't come to those who play themselves as the victim of their circumstances and let life control them instead of the other way around.

I hope this has not offended you. Believe me, that's the last thing I want to do. But you need to be aware that there is a perception out there you may need to deal with, whether it's fair or not fair. If your answer to the question was "no, I'm not a trophy kid and I've never been afraid of hard work," you'll still need to deal with the generalization that some people have.

If on the other hand, you answered, "Well I might be a trophy kid," then you will need to work on making sure you are willing to do whatever it takes to succeed in your new career.

If you think you're entitled to live the lifestyles of the rich and famous just by showing up, you're in denial. You'll be left in the dust. You've got to achieve. You've got to strive for it.

So here is my promise to you. If you practice the time honored virtue of hard work, saving your money instead of spending it like a drunken congressman, and practice the techniques described in these pages, the best trophies of life will all come your way. And when you actually earn them, when you truly deserve them, then I guarantee, those will be the best trophies you'll ever receive.

2

Clean Up Your eLife

Recently, a young professional called in sick to his office for several days in a row. So far, so good, no big deal. Unfortunately, he wasn't sick, he was lying. More unfortunately, while he was "sick" he went to a costume party dressed as a fairy, complete with pink leotard and magic wand. Most unfortunately, he posted pictures of himself at the party looking rather trashed on his Myspace page. OK, maybe these aren't unfortunate incidents, just dumb ones.

As fate would have it, his manager's attention was somehow drawn to the pictures on the employee's Myspace page. The next day, the manager sent the employee an email. It was short and succinct. The email included a copy of the picture and said, "Hope you're feeling better. You're fired. Nice wand." Oh, yeah, and by the way, the email was copied to the entire company email list.

The moral of the story? The things you post about yourself on the Internet can get you fired and can even do irreparable damage to your career. They can damage your reputation within an industry and prevent you from getting future jobs.

Events like that one are not isolated.

For instance, a few years ago, a young political consultant put an advertisement on a very provocative dating website, including a rather interesting photograph of himself demonstrating his "abilities." Not only that, he did it at the height of an election season. Well, politics can be an ugly profession (just looking at the guy's pics proved that), but once the political opposition found his date-site ad, it was on the front page for a few news cycles. I don't think he's worked in politics since.

Companies want people of good reputation representing their company. What you do outside the office DOES have an impact on how you are treated inside your office. It does not always seem right, but it is a reality. It is also lawful in some cases for you to be fired for things posted on the Internet even if those things have nothing to do with your work activities. In fact, I recently read an article about a fire chief of a small town being removed from her position for sexy poses posted on various websites, even though the pictures were taken years before her appointment as fire chief.

Internet searches of employees are the newest tool used by companies to be sure they have the best and brightest. More line managers, human resource staff, and hiring managers are using the Internet as a way to find out as much information on their employees as possible. And what they're finding is not always a good thing. Take a look at some of these story headlines pulled off the Internet:

- "Texas Probation Officer…Fired For Nude Internet Photos"
- "Teen Patriots Cheerleader Fired for Swastika Party Pics"
- "Teacher Fired Over MySpace Photo"
- "Kentucky Paramedic Beaten, Fired Following Internet Post"
- "Miss Nevada USA, Fired Over Naughty Internet Pictures"

There are hundreds of other stories out there just like this. What you put on the Internet can be there forever. The last thing you want to do is to have embarrassing pictures of you puking in a toilet at a college kegger, baring your private parts for a string of beads at Mardi-Gras or anything else like that for all to see until eternity.

So, how do you clean up your eLife?

First, do you have a personal site on a social network website, like Facebook.com, Myspace.com, etc.? If so, go through all of your pictures and postings and remove all compromising pics, foul language, disturbing logos, quotations, etc. Delete any postings or pics that may imply illegal activities. Delete postings that can be considered crude and rude. Don't forget any postings that may sound dark, rageful, or anti-social. If your manager sees that you have a tendency toward anarchy, you may not be long for your current job, much less a promotion.

You may also need to go to the pages of your friends and others in your network to see if you're tagged in pictures on their page. If you don't like what you see, then you should ask that person to please remove them from their site.

Next, check your email names and chat handles. Some of the names I've seen can be pretty, let's say, personal. For instance, if you use neuroticwitch@blahblah.com, or spankme@wahwah.com as your main personal email address, you may want to change it now that you're in the professional world.

The same goes for your IM handles. If the AOL or Yahoo world knows you as sexy_rose_bud, then it maybe time for a change. The chances of that coming back to bite you increase the more employers comb through your eLife.

Did you know texts, IMs, and chats can be saved. Just ask a former mayor of Detroit. He was sent to jail based on thousands of text messages he made to his alleged mistress. The text messages were made using Detroit-city owned devices. The wireless carrier actually had a complete history of all of those text messages saved in their database. They were brought out at trial and cemented the case against the mayor. Most people don't know it, but a lot of wireless phone companies save text messages in their company databases.

It's the same thing with IMs and Internet chat sessions. These "conversations" can be saved by either the hosting company or the people involved in the chat session. So, for instance, if you've been having a hot and steamy flirt session with one of your co-workers, you better hope it doesn't go bad…because all of those sessions could be saved and could one day end up in your boss' email inbox.

What about Youtube or other videos that you may have on-line? Have you looked through those to see if there's anything that could compromise or jeopardize your career?

What about blog posts? Have you posted extreme views on politics, gossiped about people you know, disrespected coworkers, management, clients, etc? Check it out and clean it up. You may have those feelings, but why do you feel you need the whole world to know about them?

Have you Googled yourself? I'm sure your employer has or soon will. What will they find? You would be surprised at how much is on-line about you. It could be high-school athletic performances or other types of reviews in a local newspaper. But what about an arrest for a DUI? Look, there's not much you can do about things you'll find. But you need to know what's out there and be prepared to explain it to someone who is going to ask you about it.

As an aside, there are processes in many states to allow people to apply for expungement of criminal convictions. An expungement removes all criminal records from police and court databases thereby making them unavailable for background checks. A qualified attorney can provide more information about this legal process. Of course, it is only likely to be successful for minor convictions. But in this day of heightened security concerns, any derogatory information can potentially be harmful to your career.

Remember, the Internet is a wonderful thing, but it's like a bad STD. People post the most intimate, private, and personal thoughts and images, somehow thinking that people really care and that nobody beyond their friends will ever see. But once it's out there, it may be there forever and it may have life-changing consequences.

As a new professional, one of your primary jobs is to protect your valuable reputation. Nothing at this point is more important to you than how people see you. As our society moves forward, it will be harder and harder to keep personal and professional lives separate since it is so easy to transmit images and thoughts to anyone and everyone.

Make sure you are using your eLife to post an image of responsibility, trustworthiness and professionalism.

3

Keeping Up Appearances

There was a laundry detergent commercial that ran during a recent Superbowl that featured a "talking" stain on the shirt of a young man interviewing for a job. The interviewer could not hear a word the poor guy was saying because he was so distracted by the stain. It was really funny. And it was really true. People judge you by your appearance way before they judge your workplace contribution.

It should go without saying that the first-year professional should have impeccable personal appearance and grooming habits. Unfortunately, sometimes new professionals think that an occasional unshaven face or unkempt hair will go unnoticed. This is not true. The chances are that nobody will mention it. But, take my word for it, people notice and do talk about it. Here are some other things that distract people from the inner you:

- Weak or scraggly beards and/or moustaches
- Heavy or overuse of colognes and perfumes
- Body odor of any kind (including those caused by smoking or irregular use of deodorant, or for women only, the unchecked odor of "Aunt Flow")
- Unpolished or worn-out shoes
- Unwashed hair
- Bad breath and dirty teeth
- Stained or wrinkled ties

- Clothes considered inappropriate for the workplace (especially true for women since they have WAY more options than men)
- Wrinkled shirts or suits

You get an idea of what I am talking about. If you are over fourteen, chances are your glands will require you to seriously think about taking care of body odor. This is perhaps the most offensive of the items in the above list. And it never ceases to amaze me when I am talking to someone who actually reeks of body odor. I really do not want to talk with them very long. I kind of think that smell may somehow attach to me. I know, I'm weird that way. In any event, it totally distracts me from whatever that person is saying. The last thing I want to do is to put that person out in front of a client or any customer representing my company. So, if there is any possibility you are putting out a bad odor, eliminate it.

Oh, and do not try to cover it up with body sprays or perfume. Bathing in Axe or Channel can be just as offensive to some people. Some people react to strong colognes much in the same way people react to cigarette smoke odor. Some are even allergic to some of the synthetics used in making the colognes. This does not mean don't use them; it just means don't shower in them.

Another consideration is the wrong image that you are sending out by your inability to grow hair in the intended places. A few scraggly hairs under your nose do not constitute a mustache. Remember, you want to have the image of a professional ready to represent your company to the public. You are not "flipping burgers" anymore. If it does not add maturity to your look, swallow your pride; buy a razor and shave it off.

Moving down the list of personal appearance offenses, never underestimate the negative power of ratty-looking clothes. Please note, this does not mean that you need to have an expensive wardrobe. Just keep your things neat and presentable. So, if you do not have someone who can iron your shirts like Mom did, now would be a good time to learn. And here's another tip for you cotton and linen wearers: Those wrinkles really aren't a fashion statement.

The requirements of neatness and presentability are an investment in time. Time is required on a regular basis to inspect your outfits, shirts and suits for loose buttons, stains, hanging threads, and the like. Although dry cleaning or laundering can be expensive, it may be an option if you don't have time to keep up your clothes. You may want to rotate the clothes that you bring to the cleaners so that you won't get hit with a large bill. Fifteen dollars each week may be easier to handle than sixty dollars all at once. Not only will your clothes be sharp looking, they will also last longer. Also, many dry cleaners will do alterations and repairs if you can not do them.

By the way, keeping an extra clean shirt or blouse at work is a good idea in case of a spilled cup of coffee, a mustard stain, or a nasty blotch of ink from a good pen gone wild. It is also useful if an important client or some other VIP happens to show up on Casual Friday.

Time is also required to take care of your shoes. Make sure they are polished and not scuffed up or worn out. Take time to polish or at least buff them up on a regular basis. This is the type of thing you can do while watching television or listening to your iPod. You can even do it outside while you work on your suntan. But, remember, when people are not looking in your eyes, they tend to look down. What they are seeing is your clothes and your shoes and forming subtle impressions about you based on what condition those things are in.

Now picture the final product – you are someone who is always in a clean pressed suit or outfit, with sharp shirts or blouses, and shiny shoes. Your hair is well kept, not scraggly. You smell good but not overpowering.

So, up to this point it sounds like this chapter has mostly been targeted at the guys. But ladies, you're not off the hook either.

Are you aware of what others see when you walk into the office or into a meeting? Again, this is not a book about how to dress for success, but more about giving you advise on how to create good impressions to separate you from the rest of the crowd. All the above about cleanliness and sharpness of clothes applies to you as well. But as a woman, you have a lot more clothing options than do men. For guys, it is pretty much business casual slacks and shirt. Maybe a suit and tie. But for women, the list can be business suits, skirts and blouse, sweaters, pant suits, etc. Face it, you all have way more options than do the men.

So, considering where you work, are your clothes saying about you what you want them to say? Are they telling the world that you are a serious player who is ready to take on the additional responsibility that comes with leadership? What should you be looking at? Well, in general, suffice it to say that your clothes should not be showing off your physical attributes to the detriment of your vocational skills and talents. You should check your cleavage and the length of your skirts. Chances are, if you are in a professional workplace, a bare midriff is not ever appropriate. You want to be taken seriously for the contributions you can make to the bottom line, not for how close your bottom is to the hem line. OK, sorry, that was lame.

Most people, even you and me, form opinions about others based on external appearances. So try to avoid those wardrobe distractions that may be sending out the wrong impression. Think about the guy with the bad hair piece, the gold medallion hanging around his neck and the diamond pinkie rings. Do you trust that person to give you an honest deal on a car purchase? Think about the woman with a body full of tattoos, piercings and gauges. On first impression, do you think she would have a great customer service attitude? No matter how fair or unfair it may seem, the presentation sends a message way before anything else does.

When it comes to presenting yourself in the workplace, the goal for men and women alike is the same. You want to be taken seriously. You want to be looked at as someone with advanced maturity and as someone who "gets it." You want to be looked at as someone who has a sense of self-awareness.

Just remember, before you even say "good morning" when you arrive at the office, your physical presence and appearance will go a long way toward impacting how others you work with, and work for, think about you.

4

Things Not to Do if You're a Slob

OK, so one of the major themes of this book is about putting out an image of professionalism. After all, you're a new professional and you want to act the part. But let's face it. Some people are just messy. If you recognize this about yourself, there are things you need to do to preserve all the hard work you are putting into your new professional image.

Let me start out by saying that what works for some people doesn't work for everyone. For instance, some people are "pile" people. They have a pile for everything and know exactly where in which pile everything is. If you ask them for a copy of some document, they go right to the middle of the third pile from the left and pull it out. You could call it organized chaos.

Other people are Spartan-like. They are minimalists when it comes to office clutter. You won't find a scrap of paper, a fleck of dust, a smudge on their computer screen, nothing. The thought of having a stray piece of paper on their desktop makes them extremely anxious. In fact, if they're not in their cubicle, you wonder if anyone even works in it.

Still, others are pack rats. They keep everything they've ever received. Documents, presentations, gifts, pictures of kids, trinkets, fast food wrappers, at least 4 or 5 partially filled cups, mugs or glasses, and at least a few pieces of clothing. It's all there. The only space in their cubicle that's not filled with junk is the trash can. That's perfectly empty.

So, maybe these are the extremes, but as you roam the cubicles of your office, you'll at least see variations of the above. If I had to recommend which of the above was acceptable to maintain your image as an organized and effective new professional, I would have to say to be somewhat closer to the Spartan-like and as far away as possible from the pack-rat.

If you have natural tendencies to be a rather messy or unorganized person, you're not alone. According to a February, 2006 survey by office furniture manufacturer Steelcase, Inc., 12 percent of office workers consider themselves "packrats" and another 2 percent identify themselves as "slobs."

If you consider yourself in this 14 percent group, you need to know you are risking your future growth within your company. If you acknowledge a need to be less of a mess, the three main areas to focus on improving are your appearance, your work area, and your automobile. Do you see the pattern? These are the three areas that your peers will see.

Let's start with your appearance. Keeping up your appearances is covered in the previous chapter in this book. But since it is such an important component, it is worth a quick reminder here. Even if you work in a casual dress environment, you need to take it up a notch. According to a September, 2006 survey by the on-line job placement firm Ladders.com, of the 2,245 executives surveyed, 60% thought casual dressers risked not being taken seriously. It makes sense. If you don't put out an image of total professionalism, you may seem like a fun person, but not necessarily one that is ready for more responsibility or leadership.

Next, consider your work space. If your workspace looks like the office dumpster, you are doing serious damage to your advancement opportunities. Whether it is accurate or not, the truth is that most people associate being unorganized and sloppy as being lazy. It doesn't matter how hard you work, it will be very difficult for your management to see the performance through the clutter.

Take a look at the offices and work spaces of your boss and the other managers and executives in your company. Aside from the nicer furniture and walls that may actually reach the ceiling, look at how they are organized. You need to be at least as good as they are.

So, how do you get into the habit of keeping your area clutter-free? According to the Steelcase survey, the average worker spends just over 20 minutes per day organizing their work space. That means that one way for you to start getting organized could be to actually plan it into your schedule. How about if you scheduled a 30-minute meeting for yourself everyday at 12:30 p.m.?

Use that time to be sure you have discarded all of your trash, separated and shredded or placed in the recycle bin all scrap or unneeded hard-copy documents, and sorted all remaining documents into piles that make logical sense. Then, take those piles and place them in files within the file cabinets in your work area.

Remember, not only are you going to improve your image, but you will become more efficient in being able to find items that you may later need to reference. Also, some companies have strict confidentiality and security policies that prohibit important company documents and artifacts from being left unsecured overnight.

Be sure to throw away old cups and clean and store all food containers, utensils and coffee mugs. If you have a coat and two sweaters piled on your desktop, you can fold and store them on a shelf or in a file drawer.

Finally, let's think about your car. There may come a time when you need to give a ride to coworkers or even your boss. There are even times when you may be asked to pick someone up from the airport in your vehicle, or to take someone home from an after-hours gathering. Nobody is going to expect you to be driving an expensive new car. The type of car you drive is not as important as how you maintain the one you have. If your car looks like you've been living in it for the past six months, you need to clean it up. Food wrappers and soft-drink containers, plastic bottles, old mail, whatever it happens to be, it all needs to be jettisoned. Buy a CD holder and some car storage bags so that things have a place. If someone fears they may stick to your seat after riding with you, then either clean your car or don't offer the ride. Remember, it is all about the image you want to put out to others.

Here's something to consider. Right up there with your vehicle's appearance is its reliability. Everyone runs into car issues now and then. But if your car battery dies one day making you late for work, then has a flat a few days later making you late again, the excuses are going to start wearing thin. Your boss expects you to be reliable, so your ride needs to be reliable, too.

Whether it is fair or not, people make quick and lasting decisions about others based on first impressions. That's why it matters how you dress. That's why it matters how organized your personal work area appears. That's why it matters how clean you keep your car. You know if you are in need of making improvements in how you are perceived. If you commit to making these changes, you will find a new empowerment, a new improved professional image, and a greater sense of confidence. And above all, you will increase your chances of moving to the next level of the corporate ladder.

5

How Happy Should You
Get At Happy Hour?

Pretty early in your new job, you may be invited to take part in a tradition that is as old as commerce itself – the Friday night happy hour. You now have a new group of people to get to know. And, of course, they want to get to know you better, too. So, what can be the harm? Actually, this can be a really good opportunity to bond with your new coworkers, but you must be aware of the pot holes that lay ahead.

Going to the local watering hole is a great place to learn more about the people you are working with and about the company you are working for. Many people, particularly the ones who have been with the company for a while and feel secure about their job, tend to let their hair down and reveal a side of themselves not normally displayed around the confines of the office. It can be fun to see this aspect of your workmates. Also, you can often get more information about what really goes on in your office in these informal settings that you can from any stack of memos, press releases or management meetings.

The after-hours pub scene is one that can fit very well into your career enhancement, that is, if you use the opportunity in the right way. It can be used in a subtle way to increase your reputation in the eyes of your fellow workers. But, beware. It can also be a road to self-destruction, filled with potential booby traps. You don't believe me? Then read on.

When invited to go out with the "office gang" after work, be sure to remember that people will size you up outside, as well as inside the office. Your reputation should always be protected like a precious gem. It should be guarded constantly with no time clock attached. In situations where drinking is going to be taking place, you should remember to err on the side of conservatism. Remember, your work ability may still be unproven to your coworkers or supervisor. You do not want people to attach any negative labels to you such as "he has a drinking problem" or "she seems to have a chemical dependency." You do not want to risk your future because of one drink too many.

Getting drunk with your new colleagues can do permanent damage to your career. So what are you to do? Simply put, do not get drunk. Period. I know, I know, everyone is going to call you a prude. Right? Well, maybe. But it is a small price to pay in exchange for a reputation of being serious and responsible. I understand, I understand, everyone else is drinking heavily. Why all the fuss? Well, I'm glad you asked.

First of all, this is not college anymore. You cannot drink into the wee hours and wake up with a hangover and a vague memory, if any at all, of what was said the night before. At least without consequences.

At this point in your career, it is much better to be considered a "lightweight" than a "party animal." Save your heavy partying, if you'll do it at all, to those reunions with your old college buddies, far away from the workplace, but under no circumstances with your new colleagues.

If you wake up too often with hangovers, it won't be too long before your work is affected. You may become tardy or worse, absent. And you will most certainly not be at your sharpest, most productive level if you come to work with this type of self-inflicted wound.

Also, staying sober during these occasions leaves you less likely to have loose lips or to say something that may be taken the wrong way. When someone you are with starts complaining about the boss and you agree or add to the complaints, then you have compromised yourself. In fact, there may be times when people are trying to bait you, to get you to complain or criticize. Then they might have something that they can run to the boss with. Remember, you will all wake up sober, but the things you say can never be taken back.

Staying away from alcohol will help you avoid a sort of personal blackmail where you may wonder if you said or did anything wrong last night, including the dreaded "Did I Make An Ass of Myself Last Night" Syndrome.

I realize that this is a time when you want to be accepted. The temptation to join in the fun is tremendous. But this is an important time to make the right choices and the right decisions. And, of course, there are some very blatant positive results that can come out of staying sober, as well. You may need to drive somebody home if you are the only sober one in the group. This will be remembered and appreciated for a long time. It will add to the impression that you are a socially responsible person.

Another problem with alcohol consumption with your coworkers crosses into the subject of office romances, which is addressed elsewhere in this book. But suffice it to say that not only do our lips tend to get a little looser with every drink we take; but also, our sexual inhibitions tend to be a little more liberated, as well. A little in-office flirtation, mixed with a few out-of-office drinks may lead to you and one of your new colleagues sneak off to a corner of the pub or the parking lot to start sucking face. The very last thing you want to do is to get involved in a drunken romantic fling that you will both regret just a few hours later. Although it is discussed later, office romance itself should be avoided. Drunken one-night stands with coworkers are a prescription for disaster.

So what can you do to "fit-in" without being exposed? Here are a few tips. One idea is that when you go out after hours, you can substitute tonic or soda water for a mixed drink. With a twist of lime, it looks like the real thing and nobody will be the wiser. The same thing goes for beer. Non-alcoholic brews are very popular and available in many parts of the country. So try these alternatives as a start. If people give you a hard time about it, just laugh along and say that you have some important work to do first thing in the morning and you want to be sharp. This is a good line and will be hard for anyone to argue against.

While everything you have read in this section has dealt with alcohol, I should note that these points be emphasized ten-fold when it comes to illegal drugs. Under no circumstances should you partake in illegal drug activity or use with your coworkers. This could not only be devastating to your career, but could ruin your entire life as well.

A last note before we move on. You may find a funny thing happening to you if you decide to take the challenge and follow the suggestions in this chapter. You may actually realize that you can have as much fun on these occasions without the associated negative side effects of alcohol. You may find that just being out having fun with these new people helps you attain the same good feelings or changes in your state of mind that most people use alcohol for in the first place. I'm not advocating against alcohol consumption, but you may actually realize that you don't need it to have a good time. And that would be a great personal achievement in itself!

6

Humor in the Office – Good Judgment is Everything

Do you love to make people laugh? Do you love being the center of attention? If you answered yes to either of these questions, then you'll probably find plenty of good material in the workplace. But before you treat the next team meeting like open mic night at the local comedy club, you better know how humor fits into the workplace.

Remember, first things first. You are a professional and your humor must reflect your new professionalism. If you misuse humor, you risk the chance of not being taken seriously. Remember the class clown when you were in school? He or she made everyone laugh out loud, but did you take him or her seriously? Probably not.

There is no doubt that having a good sense of humor will be an asset at your job as most people will think of you as being positive and fun to be around. They may also associate your good sense of humor with intelligence, wit and creativity.

However, with workplace humor, as with everything else, there are limits to what is appropriate and what is out of bounds. If used inappropriately, you may end up being considered obnoxious, annoying and offensive. You may be risking your chances at advancement up the ladder.

Being funny in the workplace is not at all about being able to rattle off a list of one-liners or telling good jokes. It is really more about the ability to recognize funny situations and laugh appropriately and with good taste during different circumstances.

Since every organization has its own personality, you need to understand how humor is viewed within your own company. Corporate culture rolls downhill. Consequently, the culture of your organization will largely reflect that of the senior managers and the corporate executives. So try to observe how others in your company treat humor.

Managers and supervisors all view humor differently. Some think that any sign of fun on the job means you're not being productive. Others tolerate and even enjoy working with funny people. So, get to know the sense of humor of those you work for and with.

The thing that is most important is to not let your sense of humor diminish the way you are viewed by your managers. For instance, if you are viewed as being the class clown, no matter how good your work is, you may be passed over for promotions since you may be putting out an image as being too immature or irresponsible for a bigger job.

Don't be the person who feels the need to always make a joke or a pun during a meeting. While initially cute and witty, it will eventually lead to people finding that behavior annoying and obnoxious and interrupting the flow and rhythm of the meeting. It also will lead people to think you need to be the center of attention. That in turn may cause your manager to have some concerns about your personality and ability to be a team player.

Along the same lines, try to control your laughter and try not to actually LOL too loudly. You don't want everyone walking down the halls to be thinking you and your friends are all laughs and no work. I used to work in the same cubicle row as a woman who had a very loud and distinguished laugh which could be heard throughout nearly half the floor. Though she was very capable, the feature most people associated with her was that loud cackling laugh. You don't want that happening to you.

Don't confuse your ability to make people laugh with your ability to have a professional attitude toward humor. No matter how funny you are, you always want people to know you are serious about your work.

Here are a few things to think about when committing workplace humor:

- Remember, humor is not saying something harsh to someone followed with, "I'm just kidding." That is not humor. That's just trying to be mean gift-wrapped in what you try to pass off as a joke.

- An off-shoot of that is using sarcasm as the basis of your humor. Sarcasm is generally thought of as a negative quality masking a cynical personality. That is not how you want to be perceived.

- While it should be obvious, it is useful to point out to never ever use sexual innuendo in your workplace humor. Again, while a few may laugh along, most people will find any type of sexual reference in humor unacceptable in the workplace. In fact, some may be so offended as to file a complaint to your manager. We call these kinds of incidents "HR Moments." Don't let your humor land you in an HR Moment.

- Also remember that in many workplaces, you'll be working with people from different cultures. Not only might they be from different parts of the country, but they may be from different countries altogether. Some jokes may not be at all understood by those from other cultures. In fact, some may even be offended by them.

Everyone has a different sense of humor. Some people are ok with sarcasm or dirty jokes, some aren't. The problem is in a group office setting, you never know who will be offended by what.

Face it, some people are just not funny and wouldn't recognize funny even if it hit them right in their face like a cream pie. On the other hand, some people think every meeting they attend is an opportunity to try out their stand-up routine or to show off their ability to turn a pun at every chance.

Use humor to your advantage. Use it to make people feel welcome and warm. Use it to make people know you are approachable. Use your sense of humor to build others up and you may find yourself making your way up the corporate ladder.

7

Writing Skills – Don't Leave College Without Them

In a March, 2004 survey by the National Commission on Writing for America's Families, Schools, and Colleges, good writing skills were likened to "a ticket to professional opportunity" while a lack thereof was considered a "figurative kiss of death."

One of the biggest complaints of executives about college graduates is a general lack of communication skills, particularly the inability to write effectively. This includes poor spelling and grammatical habits, as well as poor ability to structure sentences, paragraphs and complete documents.

The survey asked 120 corporate human resource directors about the importance of writing in the workplace. Interestingly, writing turned out to be one of the most highly valued "gateway" skills. According to the study, American business spends nearly $3 billion annually on training employees with poor writing skills.

"With the fast pace of today's electronic communications, one might think that the value of fundamental writing skills has diminished in the workplace," said Joseph M. Tucci, president and chief executive officer of EMC Corporation. "Actually the need to write clearly and quickly has never been more important than in today's highly competitive, technology-driven global economy."

So, what does this mean to you? Well, if you are not comfortable with writing, you are automatically limiting your ability to move up the corporate ladder. But if you are a good writer, you possess a secret weapon to help you stand out from the crowd of other rookie professionals.

How do you know if you are a bad writer? Take a look at some of these "Examples of Bad Writing" compiled by Sandra LaFave, and see if they look like anything you've written lately.

Verbosity (from Scott Adams, *The Dilbert Principle)**[*]

> "I utilized a multitined tool to process a starch resource."

> TRANSLATION: "I used my fork to eat a potato."

Density

> Existing is being unique. Existence, reality, essence, cause,
> or truth is uniqueness. The geometric point in the center
> of the sphere is nature's symbol of the immeasurable
> uniqueness within its measurable effect. A center is always
> unique; otherwise it would not be a center. Because
> uniqueness is reality, or that which makes a thing what it is,
> everything that is real is based on a centralization.[*]

Empty Words

> This change will allow us to better leverage our talent base
> in an area where developmental roles are under way and
> strategically focuses us toward the upcoming transition
> where systems literacy and accuracy will be essential to
> maintain and to further improve service levels to our
> customer base going forward.[*]

Technical Errors

> The amount of grammer and usage error's today is astounding. Not to mention spelling. If I was a teacher, I'd feel badly that less and less students seem to understand the basic principals of good writing. Neither the oldest high school students nor the youngest kindergartner know proper usage. A student often thinks they can depend on word processing programs to correct they're errors. Know way!*

* Sandra LaFave, Chair of the West Valley College Philosophy Department (http://instruct.westvalley.edu/lafave/writsamp0.htm)

So, why are people with good writing skills harder and harder to find? Well, it could be due to a poor K-12 education system that has abandoned tried and true methods of teaching this subject in favor of the latest fads.

Or it could be because for many of us, formal writing is being replaced by emailing and texting in which grammar and rules are, well, tossed out the window. I remember when HAND meant the thing on the end of your arm, not "Have a Nice Day." Since texting is here to stay, it means you need to take extra care to be sure your formal workplace writing is not polluted by your informal text or email writing. Of course, that's JMO.

There are two really easy things you can do to improve the quality of your writing. First, use a spell check available on most word processors. Second, and I know this sounds like a given, but actually read what you write before you press "send."

Spell checkers are easy to use and will also often make suggestions on grammar in addition to spelling. However, they're not foolproof. For instance, "former President Jimmy Carter" and "farmer President

Jimmy Carter" will both pass most spell checkers. But, unless the
subject is the former president's peanut farming days, the latter usage
may cause a bit of confusion for your reader.

The second suggestion is to read what you write. Sounds simple
enough, but I can't tell you how many emails and other written
communications I've received where it is very obvious the sender did
not proofread the material. It's not only about misspellings, but just
sentences that don't make sense at all.

So, how do you get better at writing? Since there are plenty of
options it's actually not too difficult to gain good writing skills. One
alternative is to search the Internet for business writing tips and
tricks. I could list some URLs here, but it would be a lot easier for
you to do a search for "business writing tips" or something similar.
You'll find a lot of sites to choose from.

The most effective approach would be to take a business writing
course at a local community college or at an on-line university. I
know you just graduated and the last thing you want to do is take
another course. But it is that important, so don't pass it up. And
don't forget, a lot of companies will reimburse you for the tuition;
it's a no-lose proposition.

Do a real gut check on your writing skills. If they are not what
they should be, do something about it. You would not want to let
something so easily fixed let you be so easily passed by.

8

Note Writing and
the Road to the Presidency

An effective technique in promoting your image with others is to regularly send personalized hand-written notes to business and personal associates. This includes thank you notes to the person who referred a new customer to your business or the vendor who invited you to a holiday party. This also includes a note to a secretary or a clerk who helped you get your work done before the deadline. You may rightfully think that it is a part of their job, but this type of recognition costs you little and goes a long way toward building a relationship that you may depend on in the future.

A personal note shows that you really cared enough to take the time to recognize the efforts of others. It is a great morale and pride builder and adds a touch of class to your work. It is important to recognize the kindness and the efforts of the people with whom you are in contact, whether it be a customer, vendor or fellow employee. Think of how it would make you feel to get a note of appreciation from a customer or fellow worker. Well, if it would make you feel good and appreciated, it will most likely have the similar effect on others.

The best way to develop this habit is to buy a box of simple thank you notes or plain cards. They do not have to be fancy or expensive. Likewise, they should not be too "cutesy" or in any way detract from your professionalism. Keep some in your briefcase and in the desk drawer in your workspace. You may even want to keep some in your vehicle's glove compartment and at your home, maybe in the nightstand next to your bed. This way you will always have them at your disposal and can make good use of idle time writing and sending them out. Of course, having a supply of stamps handy will also be helpful.

Now that you have your cards and stamps available at your fingertips, there is no reason why you should not be able to write things like:

Dear Mark,

Thank you for the wonderful job you did preparing that file. I realize it was short notice, but you really helped me get out of a bind and I appreciate your efforts.

Jane

or,

Dear Sarah,

Thank you for inviting me to the open-house at your new office. It was a pleasure meeting your coworkers and some of your other customers. I also enjoyed hearing some of the "horror stories" about getting the office opened on time. Apparently, your hard work paid off – the place looks great!

Mark Smith
XYZ Products

A common trait shared by most presidents of the United States is the many hours spent sending out these types of personal notes to people they meet throughout their busy schedules. It is one technique they use to build loyal followings among the nation's, and the world's for that matter, politically powerful.

Now I don't know if you have presidential aspirations of the political kind. But I do know that if writing personal notes helped them get to the top, it most certainly will help you.

Telephone Power

One of the most important tools in the professional world, regardless of the business you are in, is the telephone. It is important because of the power it provides the user. With the telephone you can make contact with nearly anyone, anytime, anywhere. I would venture to say that more business deals are closed over the telephone than face-to-face; that more money is made and exchanged over the telephone than is done face-to-face; that more careers are molded and developed over the telephone than they are face-to-face.

The proper use of the telephone, whether the one tied to your desk or the one stuffed in your pocket, provides you with one of the biggest challenges in your new career. With the telephone you have the power to communicate and distribute vast amounts of information to many people. But remember, you also have the power to interrupt people during their meetings or work times or to interrupt their train of thought about whatever it is they are working on. You also have the ability to delay someone from leaving the office on time in the evening or leaving the office to get to lunch. With the telephone, you have the ability to make either a good positive impression or to annoy or inconvenience someone.

In the overall communication "package," things like eye-contact, firm hand-shake and the like, are critical elements. But, remember that over the telephone, people can only hear you. Your looks, personal appearance and body language are completely irrelevant. On the phone, you must use your best skills to overcome the inability to use your other senses. Fortunately, there are things you can do to enhance your telephone power.

First, "smile" when talking on the telephone. When you smile, you actually feel better. Go ahead and try it. Didn't that feel good? That smile will come across on the telephone. Have you ever heard someone on the other end of the phone and they just sounded happy? Didn't it make you feel comfortable with them? Start developing the smile habit on the phone and you'll notice more people will be happy to get your call.

Do not mumble, nor speak too rapidly. Do not use slang. Give the person on the receiver your complete attention – anything less would be rude. Also, do not eat while on the phone – we can actually hear you chewing.

Do not try to cover your lack of experience with industry jargon that may not yet be completely familiar to you. You might get called on it if you are talking to someone with more experience than you.

Maintain good posture while speaking on the telephone. If you are slouching or reclined, it will come across in your tone of voice or your attentiveness to the person on the other end of the receiver.

If at all possible, call people during times when you feel that the other person will not be pressed for time. Of course, the circumstances and purpose of your telephone call will usually dictate when a call to a customer, peer, vendor or supervisor is appropriate. For instance, do not schedule a "getting to know you" or "just wanted to say 'Hi'" type of phone call right before or during lunch hours or right before closing time. And always remember what time it is in the time zone to which you are calling. Of course, if you have a critical piece of information that must be communicated immediately, by all means pick up the phone and do it.

Commonly, the busiest time periods for most executives are between
9:00 a.m. and 11:00 a.m. and between 1:30 p.m. and 4:00 p.m.
These are the times when the phones are the busiest, as well. Again,
there is no "best" time for an important message. You will have to use
your best judgment as to the importance and, therefore, the timing
of your phone calls.

Keep and file (electronically or in a file folder), all phone message
"While You Were Out" slips. In addition, create and maintain a
telephone log. A telephone log will help you keep an on-going record
of your contacts with clients, other employees, etc. Keep it simple.
All it needs to be is a small notebook that you keep by the phone or
in your briefcase. You just need to log the date and time of the call,
who you talked to, and what you discussed. For example, a log entry
might look like this:

> "11/30/09 – Called Tom Smith about
> the XYZ sale. He mentioned they
> received the information I sent and will
> need a week to review. We agreed that I
> should call him back next Tuesday."

If you get a message, put it in the log, and then indicate when you
called them back. If you get their voice mail or had to leave a message,
note that down. In that way, if the person calls you back, or if your
boss asks why you never returned that person's phone call, you have a
written record at hand. Believe me, you will build instant credibility
with your management if you keep a phone log.

Return phone calls promptly – even if, and especially if, you have
reasons for not wanting to make a call. This is especially true in
situations like when your boss calls about your overdue report or
when you need to return a customer's call only to tell them that they
have been rejected for a loan.

Again, document the time and results of the phone call either on the message note or in your telephone journal. For instance, write:

"12/01, 12:15 p.m. – busy," or
"12/02, 8:30 a.m. – out of office, left message with secretary," or
"12/01, 2:00 p.m. – spoke with Tom; requested files to be returned today."

Your phone log will give you an on-going record of a major part of your business. It will give you a reference library for all of your telephone communications. This will be important for you in many ways as you will have at your finger tips a complete history of some very significant business communications.

Now for a few words about your cell phone. Each workplace may have its own protocol or attitude about the use of personal cell phones. But use good judgment about how and when you use your own cell phone. Try to make your calls away from workplace areas. Check your ringer. You might find it to be stylish, cute, trendy or whatever. Other people might find it loud, obnoxious, annoying or immature. The best approach is to put it on vibrate when you get to work.

Going into a meeting, don't just put the ringer on vibrate, turn it off. Better yet, turn off the phone completely. Put it into your pocket. I once had a manager who would completely stop a meeting when he heard someone's cell phone ring. Yes, the idea was to embarrass the person about creating this interruption into the business meeting.

If you are awaiting a very important phone call, you can tell the person you are meeting with that you may need to take the call. And, of course, if you are in a job that requires you to be available for some type of emergency support, then everyone will understand. But if you need to keep your telephone on, you must still make the person or people you are meeting with your top priority.

If you need to participate in a meeting on your cell phone while traveling, try to use your mute button as much as possible in order to keep the noise factor down for the others on the call. Also, if you make or receive calls on your cell phone while driving and you need to write things down, you should by all means pull over. Talking, writing and driving just don't mix.

Finally, when away from the office and talking business on your cell phone, be aware of who is around you. Conversations you have with others may be overheard. Be sure to not allow any sensitive or classified corporate information to be heard by others lurking within earshot. Along the same lines, publicly complaining on your cell phone about your company, your boss, coworkers, etc. may put you in a compromised position if overheard by the wrong ears. So, take caution.

Remember, the telephone is a very, if not the most, powerful business tool at your disposal. Use your telephone power and your best judgment to become a more effective professional.

10

Bored Meetings

Business meetings may be one of the most important times for you to make your professional mark. The exposure you get in a meeting will have a direct impact in how others see you. These gatherings are the melting pots of business. They are the areas in which professionals from all facets of your business come together to get acquainted, exchange ideas, solve problems, and the like. These are opportunities where company meets customer, where company meets competitor, and where department staffs meet department staffs. Many first and lasting impressions are made here.

Meetings as discussed in this section are not just those conducted in your company's conference rooms. Business meetings occur any time you interact with a person or persons to conduct business. This includes your customer's conference rooms, a teleconference or video conference, a cocktail party, or a training seminar at an off-site location. These can be formal or informal. The concept of business meeting even applies to a simple telephone call.

Anytime you are in contact with someone for business purposes, you should be highly aware of the subtleties of the interaction. Although it may not be immediately apparent, you will be appraised as to your preparedness, posture, speech, appearance, attentiveness, presentation skills, thinking ability, listening skills, and, well, you get the picture. It is not enough to say the right things. It is how the whole package, that means you, gets delivered.

Here are some tips for successful business meetings for those inexperienced in the art...

- Always show up early.
- Never, ever be late without a really good reason. If you will be late, notify the meeting organizer ahead of time. Don't leave them guessing or delaying because of you.
- Be well prepared. Be familiar with the discussion topic and all pre-meeting handouts.
- Maintain good posture.
- Unless you can really add something to the conversation and are sure about what you are going to say, keep your thoughts to yourself. Remember the old adage, "it is better to be thought a fool than to speak and remove all doubt."
- Pay attention. You may be asked a question or to comment. You do not want to be caught daydreaming.
- If you are directly asked to comment on a particular issue, stick to the matter at hand. Be direct and concise in your answer. As Shakespeare's admonished "brevity is the soul of wit."
- Also, if asked to comment, stick to the facts of the issues and not the personalities of the people involved.
- To fight boredom, take notes. This will keep you actively interested in the speaker. By all means, do not fall asleep. Fight it by taking long deep breathes. I do not know how many meetings I've attended where people start nodding off in front of the whole group. If there was ever a moment meant for Youtube or America's Funniest Home Videos, it is watching someone slowly nodding off during a business meeting.

10

How Late Will You Stay?

One of the best ways to show your manager an "I'm all in" type of attitude is to respect your working hours. While the official hours for your company or department might be 8:00 to 5:00 p.m., the "unofficial" work hours may be more like 7:45 a.m. to 5:15 p.m.

The longer you work with your company, the more you will notice what those unofficial work hours are. If your expected start time is 8:00 a.m., don't be surprised to find people straying in to the office as late as to 9:00 a.m. Likewise, if quitting time is 5:00 p.m., a quick look out the window will show you that the parking lot starts thinning out at about 4:30 p.m.

The people who pinch their working hours are usually considered coasters or skaters. They are just happily going along their merry way with no particular desire to get ahead. Of course, if you want to move ahead, you won't copy their style. Just say no to the "Nine-to-Five" approach to your work life.

A good rule of thumb to follow is to be at your office at least 15 minutes early and stay 15 minutes later on a consistent basis. Another approach some people take is to be there 5 minutes before the boss gets there and stay for 5 minutes after he or she leaves.

The point is that the only way to get noticed in your workplace is to be there. And when you're there, you need to stand out. Showing up early and staying late will help you get attention that the late strollers just won't get. You will find that just by following these rules, your manager will consider you a hard worker who is "always there when needed."

On a similar matter, don't be afraid to put in overtime, if approved, even if it is simply to observe how another department does their work. Again, during OT hours, you have a better time being noticed by those executives who are themselves in the office after hours. These are often opportunities to get to know your managers a little better and to forge personal relationships with them. If you are frequently seen in the office putting in the extra effort, your star will rise much more quickly than those who are not willing to make that commitment.

A certain amount of overtime should be a part of your normal work schedule. Just ink it into your calendar. Practice it and get used to it. You'll find that those early morning or early evening hours are great times to get meaningful work done. There are no interruptions, no telephones and no meetings to attend.

By showing your dedication, hard work and commitment, your management will give you opportunities to move up. And since you are already practicing this approach to your work hours, you will already be used to the time demands that may likely come from your new responsibilities.

Working late may also present some other interesting opportunities to get noticed. Once, while working in a loan office for a major bank, we had just closed several loans that meant a lot of income to our new office. We put many hours of work into completing the seeming mountain of required paperwork. The documents needed to be sent out that night by overnight courier.

The office manager's normal routine was to place all outgoing overnight mail stacked on the floor next to her desk. In hindsight, that was a pretty dumb place to put important packages. But, strangely enough, that's how we did it. Unfortunately, it was also close enough to the waste basket that the afternoon cleaning crew mistook it for trash and, as is their duty, they removed it along with the other office garbage.

As it turns out, one of our regional VPs was visiting the office for a few days. Just before he was ready to leave for the evening, he asked where the loan documents were. After confirming that the courier had not picked them up, we determined that the janitorial crew put them in the trash. By this time, they were likely already in one of the massive dumpsters that served the entire office park.

Since I was there late, I was able to volunteer for a rather dirty job. I offered to get on some old clothes and jump into the dumpsters to search for the loan documents. Of course, the offer was accepted and I started my dumpster diving. Unfortunately, although I searched for hours into the night, I never did find the documents and we had to start the entire process over again.

What did happen though was that I received many notes, some extremely funny, from quite a few of this major corporation's senior executives, including its president. This happened during my first year after graduating college and it was a great way to get noticed all the way up the ladder. It would not have happened had I left at 5:00 p.m.

I know that working overtime or putting in extra hours does put a crimp in your personal or social life. But at this point in your life, if you are serious about advancement, you should really be career-oriented. Many people can make rapid jumps up the corporate ladder in their first five years of employment. Being considered an employee willing to put in the extra hours is a great way to do just that.

12

Open Your Brag File

OK…we all know it's not polite to brag. At least most of the time. But it is always a good idea to keep a brag file. A brag file is simply a file where you list or store samples of everything you have accomplished on your job or in other parts of your life. The idea of keeping such a file may seem a bit narcissistic, but if done correctly, it can be a great personal advancement tool.

There are at least two very good reasons to keep a brag file.

First, and most important, at some point in your new job, you will likely be asked to participate in some kind of annual performance review. During the review, you will be asked to cite and discuss your contributions to the company. You may be asked to list your accomplishments, strengths, weaknesses, etc.

Sure, telling someone about all the great things you've done may sound easy enough. And you should be given at least a couple of weeks to prepare your list. But putting it together may be more difficult than you think. It's hard enough to remember all of the things you did over the last two weeks, let alone over the last year.

In fact, why don't you try doing just that right now. Think of at least five things you've accomplished over the last two weeks. Seriously, stop reading and think about five things you've gotten done in the last 14 days. OK, how about three things. Hmmm...how about just one thing. Not as easy as you thought, huh?

I remember the pressure I felt during my first annual performance review. I knew there was a raise coming, but I did not know how much it would be. My manager gave me a form to complete and asked me to list my accomplishments for each of the last 4 quarters. I was dumbfounded and didn't know where to start. I knew I had accomplished all kinds of things. In fact, I knew I had worked rings around most of my coworkers. I just could not for the life of me put together a list of them all.

I ended up getting a middle-of-the-road assessment and not much of a raise. But I did learn a great lesson. For the rest of that year, and for the rest of my career, I've kept a very simple file of everything I've done. Projects completed, sales made, articles written by me, articles written about me, conferences attended, classes taken, awards received...they are all in there.

Over the years, whenever I needed to prepare for a review, compete for a position, or even give myself a mental boost, I just pull out the old brag-file.

There is one other important reason for you to create your brag file and that is to prepare your resume. If you have a list of all of your accomplishments and achievements available at your fingertips, then you will have much more detail available when selling your abilities to future prospective employers.

So, go ahead and brag...just keep it to yourself.

13

Keeping Abreast

Some people are news junkies and love to keep up with current events and the world around them. I'll bet if you go up to them and ask them anything from who's the Secretary of State to what is the state of Hollywood, they'll be able to offer an opinion.

If that describes you, then great. Keep it up. But if you haven't developed an interest in knowing what's going on in the world, now is definitely the time to start.

Not only will you be able to carry on a conversation about what is going on with your job, you'll also be interesting when conversations turn to other topics outside the office.

But keeping abreast of your surroundings at this point in your life needs to go way beyond awareness of the headlines. While that will make you interesting at the office cocktail party, there are other things you should be researching to make you more valuable to your company.

You need to take every opportunity to research your company, your industry and your competitors. You need to understand the history of your industry, how your company was formed and how it developed into its current organization.

You may be in the IT or sales organization of your business, but you should still be aware of your company's mission, goals and objectives. You should keep track of your company's product and service offerings. You should be aware of how those products and services are delivered to customers. Does your company offer its products through retail, over the Internet, via mail-order?

You should also know where in the world your company operates and what they do in those locations. For instance, is your corporate administrative headquarters in San Jose, your IT development in Las Vegas, Nevada and Chennai, India and your main operations headquartered in Orlando?

What are your company's main lines of business? Who are the main executives managing each of those businesses? What are their backgrounds? How valuable would it be to know that the head of product development is a member of the same sorority as you? Wouldn't you like to know that the vice president of Finance went to the same college as you? These are little pieces of knowledge that might be very helpful when it's time for promotions.

The Internet offers many ideas and suggestions on how to research your industry and company. The most comprehensive website I have found is one offered by Polson Enterprises. Its website is: http://www.virtualpet.com/industry/howto/search2.htm#companies

As you will see, there is no lack of information available to gain knowledge about your business and competitors. The problem may very well be that there is too much information. So don't overwhelm yourself digging through all of the information.

Remember, the goal of this book is to arm you with tips and tricks that will set you apart from the other new professionals with whom you are competing for those few promotional opportunities. Your research should go that deep. You should learn enough to be able to display that you have knowledge beyond your specific job and

a well-rounded understanding of how your company works and
makes money. You should learn enough about the people who run
your business so that you understand their background and their
corporate philosophy. You should learn enough to know what new
products or technologies your competitors are deploying in order to
offer that up to your own management.

Now, imagine the look on everyone's face when your manager asks
your team about some new technology that is being considered by
the company and you are able to rattle off what that technology is,
who else in the industry is using it and what their results are. Believe
me, if you are able to do that, you will definitely be set apart from
your peers.

Part 2

Intangibles

14

Losing the Blame Game

Have you ever heard of the Blame Game? It happens all the time and has probably been happening since the beginning of time. In fact, in the Bible, the Blame Game started in the Garden of Eden. You may have heard the story. God tells Adam and Eve they can have anything they want in the garden, with the exception of the forbidden fruit. Well, one day a snake convinces Eve to eat the forbidden fruit. She then convinces Adam to do the same. Next thing you know paradise is lost. When God questions Adam, he responds with something like, "Hey, don't blame me, this woman You gave me made me do it." When God turns to Eve, she says, "Hey, don't blame me. The snake made me do it."

You get it? Even though both of them knew the right thing to do, and had clear instructions about what not to do, they did it anyway. Instead of being accountable for their actions, they decided to blame everything else but themselves.

But the Blame Game is not just limited to a story in the Bible. The game is played every day, by people in every element of society, whether it's a student who blames the dog for eating his homework or the employee who blames her coworker for missing an important deadline.

The Blame Game has many forms and may also be known as finger pointing and good excuses. Most managers think excuses are like rear-ends: everyone's got one and they all stink.

You will also recognize the game in phrases that sound like, "look what you made me do," "poor-poor me," or as in Bart Simpson's case, "Don't blame me, I didn't do it."

No matter what you call it, the bottom line for all of these is that commitments get made and broken without the responsible person having enough personal integrity to admit and accept the blame and take ownership.

So, what happens when you play the Blame Game in the work place? Here's a list:

- You'll be considered unreliable or undependable because you're never on time and you've always got an excuse.
- You may get a reputation that it always takes you more time than others to complete tasks.
- You may be thought to have trouble focusing or not skilled enough to perform your tasks.
- You may need to beware of the people you are blaming who may seek revenge for always being blamed for your missed deadlines.

None of the above are impressions you want your bosses to associate with you.

Conversely, what may happen when you actually refuse to play the Blame Game?

- You'll be known as one who has the courage and guts to accept responsibility when things don't always go right.
- You will be known as being a protector and one who is loyal to others on the team.
- You will be considered to have personal integrity.
- You will earn respect from coworkers and managers.

Now, please note, if you are perpetually missing deadlines, no amount of owning the blame will insulate you from getting in trouble with your management. A deadline is a deadline, not a suggestion. You still have to perform. If you are going to miss a deadline, notify your manager sooner than later. Don't just miss it and create surprises for other people who are depending on your completed work.

The reality is that in the workplace, there are always a lot of interdependencies. People count on you as much as you count on other coworkers, outside vendors, equipment, process, etc. to get your jobs done. A breakdown with any of those dependencies can hamper your ability to complete your assignments.

So, if you are truly having trouble getting your work done and it is truly attributable to outside factors, there is a way to deal with it. First, try to recognize the problems early and document them. Then communicate them to your manager and others who might be affected. Don't wait until after you've missed a deadline to inform your boss. Shout loud and shout early if you run into problems.

For instance, if you have a deadline approaching to install a piece of software on the computers for the marketing department, but you have not yet received the software from the software company, then you should immediately send an email to your manager letting him or her know about the potential delay and what you've done to try to avoid it. For instance, indicate that you've made telephone calls and have sent emails to the vendor requesting project status or reasons for the delay. Also include other details such as when the new estimated time of arrival of the software is. Finally, include the action that you are requesting from your manager, such as "Can you please contact the software company manager to determine if a faster delivery date is available?"

You may also want to notify others who may be impacted by the delay (like those in the marketing department) by not having that software. Your manager can help to decide what other communication is appropriate.

Effective leaders accept blame for their own actions and for the actions of those they manage. They also recognize and communicate problems sooner rather than later. Not participating in the Blame Game is essential to moving up a notch on the corporate ladder. It's one game you don't want to play.

15

Goofing Up and the Art of the Apology

Mistakes happen. It is inevitable. At some point in your new career, you're going to make an honest, legitimate mistake. Maybe you transposed a number on a spreadsheet. Maybe you thought someone said they needed your design completed by the 21st, but you thought they said the 25th.

If you are faced with the situation where you've not met someone's expectations and it's your fault, there are three things you need to do. Just own it, apologize for it, and fix it.

There is no rocket science in any of these three things. But I want to spend a few minutes discussing the importance of the apology.

Have you noticed what many people do when it's discovered they've made a mistake? Usually, the first thing that people do when they are called out on a mistake is try to make an excuse or blame someone else. People are fearful that you'll get mad or they'll get in trouble or fired or whatever. Some people just have a lot of arrogance and can't get themselves to admit to others that they're less than perfect. They just have trouble admitting they goofed up.

So, if it happens to you, you need to swallow your pride and own it.

That's the first step.

But have you also noticed that even if people acknowledge a mistake, you hardly ever hear an apology? Let me tell you why it's important to apologize. A former client of mine was telling me about a transaction gone badly at a retail store. I'll spare you the details, because it's his reaction that is key. He told me, "It wasn't so much that the error occurred, but that nobody was willing to apologize, to simply say, 'We're sorry.' It became a matter of principle and of where my next purchase was going to be; certainly not with them."

His reaction is critical to understanding why you must acknowledge ownership of the problem and then apologize for the error. Not only does the apology pacify the victim, but it lets them know you care. It also may help keep them a customer of your service, whether you are an accountant, a retailer or an advertising shop.

So, the second step is to apologize. Believe it or not, just those few words, "That was my fault, I am sorry" will go a long way in keeping you in a favorable light with your manager.

Finally, offer to go the extra distance to help rectify the situation. Swallow your pride and do whatever is necessary to make it right for the customer. If you messed up, you need to fix it. It is just the right thing to do. Look, mistakes happen (hopefully not too frequently). It's how you fix it, along with the attitude you fix it with, that makes all the difference.

Don't expect any accolades for fixing something you broke in the first place, even though sometimes, when an employee turns a bad situation into a good one, the word gets around. But you can be sure that when an employee takes a bad situation and does nothing, that will make its way to management.

16

Promises, Promises –
Is the Check Really in The Mail?

There is one thing that will keep you out of trouble, let you work with a clear conscience, and also, by the way, let you sleep well at night. That is to always keep your promises and to communicate when a promise you made may not be fulfilled.

In an article titled "Promise-keeping: A Low Priority in a Hierarchy of Workplace Values" published in the Journal of Business Ethics (Volume 27, Number 4 / October, 2000), a study of 700 individuals concluded that the notion of keeping a promise was the lowest of business place core values. The study's participants "overwhelmingly ignored their promises even when legally bound to keep them." In the scenarios presented, only 30% of the participants lived up to their promises. Even when the participants were told they were legally required to keep their promise, only 57% followed through.

WHAT AN OPPORTUNITY FOR YOU! Remember, the premise of this book is to give you opportunities to develop habits that will set you apart from your peers.

The natural human condition, at least in most cases, is to avoid conflict. Most people want to please their managers or customers. When your supervisor asks if you can deliver the report by the end of the day, the natural reaction is to say yes. When a customer wants to know if her package is going to be shipped this week, the natural reaction is to say yes. Saying yes is quite often the path of least resistance. It is the quickest way to get a positive and satisfying reaction from your customer. You say yes, they get happy. That's a pretty simple formula.

But what happens when things go south and the promise you made won't be met? The deadline is approaching and you know you won't be able to make it. What do you do then?

Well, before answering that question, let's start by looking at the promise you made in the first place. When you made the commitment, did you honestly believe that it could be met? Did you know you had enough time in your day to meet the "I'll have the report completed by the end of the day" promise you made to your boss? Did you know if the shipping department had all the information necessary to get the package to your customer's location by the end of the week?

If the answers to these questions are "No," then you've already set yourself up for failure. So, why did you say "Yes" with your mouth, when in your head you knew "No" was the right answer? Most likely, it's because it was easier or because you didn't want to look incompetent, especially as the new guy or gal on the team, or because you didn't want to lose the customer to a competitor. Those are all natural and normal responses. But if you know it can not be done by the requested date, you owe it to yourself, your customer and your employer to give a straight answer.

And here's where saying "no" actually will build your credibility. Let's take the example of your manager asking you to complete the report by the end of the day. If you know you have two other projects that you are already working on with similar urgency attached, explain that to your manager. Ask her for her advice about your priorities. That is one of the reasons why you have a manager. Let them know your challenges and also let them know your flexibility. That may mean offering to work a few hours extra in the evening to get the work done. It may mean that you can come in earlier the next day. If you give her options, not only will she likely help rearrange your work activities, but you will also be shown to have a great work attitude where flexibility matters.

What about making a commitment that you thought you could keep, but when push came to shove, things fell apart? Look, things happen. You may have made the promise based on ideal conditions. But many times these conditions are out of your control. Unfortunately, you get caught holding the bag. For instance, with your loan customer, maybe the loan officer had all the information to make a timely decision, but he had a family emergency that took him out of the office for a few days. What should you do then?

Well, you could just ignore it and hope he gets back in time to meet the deadline to which you've committed. Or you could wait until the customer calls you on Friday to find out the status and deliver the news at that time. Or you could try to contact the loan officer, or his or her manager, explain your dilemma, get a new estimated approval time, and call your customer right away with the new ETA and the reason for the delay. The customer may not like the answer (and may express it with a lot of emotion), but will in the end appreciate your honesty and communication. So will your manager for that matter. And that will set you apart.

By the same token, when you say you will take an action, do it. Don't put it off. There's an old idiom "the check is in the mail." But it's usually accompanied with a wink and a nod and the sarcastic notion of "yeah, right." You don't want people to think of you as a "check in the mail" kind of person. When you say you are going to do something, do it right then if possible. Putting "something in the mail" or emailing a document to a coworker, or returning a phone call by 3:00 p.m. are all types of promises that you need to keep.

So, the bottom line on promises is this. Don't make promises you know you can't keep. If you do make a promise, do everything you can to deliver on it. And if at some point it looks like you can not make good on your commitment, get as much information you can as to why you cannot make it and communicate to all involved parties as soon as possible.

17

Personal Problems = Personal Life

Your boyfriend broke up with you, your car is having trouble, you can't make rent, blah, blah, blah. Everyone has problems. But the likely truth is that nobody really cares about your problems since they've got so much to deal with in their own lives. I know that sounds harsh. But it's the truth. And it is one of the reasons you need to avoid bringing your personal problems into your professional life.

Let's face it. It's not about IF you'll have personal issues. It's about WHEN you'll have personal issues. So, accept that as you go through life, things will happen in your "outside the office" world that will cause you distress, distraction and disappointment.

As difficult as it will be, you need to avoid bringing your personal problems to the office. Not as easy as it sounds, I know. Many of us are emotional beings and often times find it hard to mask our true emotions from the outside world. It's also hard to totally compartmentalize one part of our lives from another. But you've got to try to do it and here's why.

The last emotion you want to evoke from your peers and supervisors is pity. Showing up to work with an out-of-control personal life, a constant black cloud hanging over your head, or an "if it weren't for bad luck I'd have no luck at all" kind of life will cause people to pity you. While it may feel comforting for people to look at you and say, "You poor thing," it is also the seed that leads to people looking at you as a weak and unreliable coworker.

Constant pity will eventually lead you to suffer the loss of respect of your peers and managers. You will be at an extreme disadvantage when promotional opportunities arise if you are perceived as having too much stress or being too emotionally weak to handle additional responsibilities.

A friend of mine told me of a man with whom she works who was experiencing financial difficulties. For a period of time, he was often on his desk phone with his creditors explaining about his problems with the IRS and paying his daughter's college tuition, as well as his son's problem with gambling. My friend tells me the guy is very likeable and capable, but was also passed over for a promotion because of the concern he was not able to handle the pressure that came with the position.

Trust me, most managers will understand about your own legitimate illnesses or the illness or passing of a loved one. They will also find some leeway in a divorce. But even those circumstances have their limits. As difficult are these situations, there is an expectation that you will deal with them appropriately and then move on with life and with work.

Most certainly, a break-up or fight with a boyfriend or girlfriend or generally any similar relationship type problems are not suitable for workplace discussion.

The reality is that people who always come to your cubicle with problems are not welcome guests. I have witnessed a situation where one person would go to anyone who would listen to her talk about her relationship problems. She had no problem walking into everyone's work area and just start going on and on about the latest argument, the latest "why can't he commit to me" complaints, and the "you'll never guess what he did this time."

Although people gave her the impression that they cared, she was soon a part of the office grapevine. In fact, it was not long before people were avoiding her at all costs. This poor girl was not only looked at as annoying, but also as a poor worker, even though her work was generally done pretty well. It was simply that people had the impression she spent more time gossiping about her personal life, than she did working. She also took work time away from other people who really needed to meet their own deadlines.

On the other hand, I have also experienced the situations where coworkers have lost loved ones, even in the most tragic ways. Those who were able to work through the problems without letting them creep into their work lives were by far highly productive and well-thought of.

What made them effective at work while dealing with a rough personal time was the existence of an out-of-office support structure. For some, it is family. For others it is a good friend or group of friends to share the burden. And others dealt with their problems by getting involved in other activities through their church or volunteer groups that took their minds off of their problems. Personally, I feel that volunteering to help others in need is the quickest way to see that my problems are not so bad at all.

Finally, if you don't have any other support group outside of work to lean on, there are a few things that you might consider.

First, check your benefits package or call your human resources department to find out if your company offers an Employee Assistance Program (EAP). Many times, these programs offer some type of confidential counseling service free of charge to the employee. If it is part of your benefits, take advantage of it.

Second, you may want to seek a professional counselor on your own.

Again, it is the same concept as the EAP. Be sure to check your health care coverage as some mental health services are covered under your health benefits. Otherwise, you will need to prepare to pay cash for these services.

If you find you are having trouble fulfilling your job duties because you are distracted by your personal problems, you do have one other option. You can consider using personal, sick or vacation time to gain control of the situation. Sometimes a day or two away from the stresses of life gives you the chance to gain a clear perspective on what need to be your life's priorities. Be sure your boss knows ahead of time that you'll be taking that time off. Do not just blow off work. But if it will make you a better worker, taking a "mental health day" is often just what is needed.

18

Office Romances

Let's face it; most relationships don't turn into marriage. That's why people normally date different people over a period of time. Then maybe at some point, if we've met the right one, we make that long-term commitment. There is supposed to be a many-to-one relationship between dating and the long term commitments that lead to marriage. You date many people, but very few end up being solid long-term relationships. So with the odds of most relationships NOT working, why would you want to have one with someone you work with?

A failed office relationship may create an awkwardness that can affect your ability to perform. Think about it. You date for a while. You tell each other some secrets. One person develops really strong feelings for the other. Then boom, there's a break-up. It's bad enough dealing with that outside the office. But what if it's a person sitting in the cubicle right next to you? Oh, yeah, that's a lot of fun. How will you react when you start getting funny little looks as you pass someone in the hall...or the chuckle that turns into a straight-face when you walk into the break room? I know in TV-land, relationships like these can work out. But you happen to be living in real life.

The hard reality is that your new job may mean you are in an area far from home where you don't know anyone outside of work. You may get very lonely from time to time. The office is a natural place to meet people with similar interests and after spending 40 or 50 hours a week with a person you may think you know them pretty well. On top of that, after a long week, there's just not a lot of time to meet other quality people. That's still not a good enough reason to deal with the absolute awkwardness and aftermath of a failed relationship with a coworker.

If you think it's hard enough running into an ex in the grocery store, the gym or at one of the local clubs, how bad will it be when you have to go to the same meetings, work on the same projects, or walk down the same hallways with your ex?

It's even worse when that person you're dating is your boss. Imagine how it will be when it comes time for your performance review? How is THAT going to go? What if you are really a great worker, but she gives you an average grade to avoid the appearance of impropriety? Well, that sucks, but boy you're lucky to be dating her.

What if you actually get a big raise or a promotion based on your merits? Do you think people would actually believe it was just due to your work performance or the fact that you are dating your boss?

Staying out of office romances is another way to keep your name out of the office gossip mill. Believe it or not, office relationships never remain a secret. People are very perceptive about these things and will pick up on the dynamics between the two of you.

But what if you are so good at keeping your relationship out of the limelight, then you notice someone flirting with your girlfriend or boyfriend? After all, isn't that how your relationship started? How will you deal with that?

Finally, there may actually be legal complications arising out of a failed office relationship. The whole notion of sexual harassment is very real with charges being leveled against both male and female co-workers. A failed office relationship can put both you and your company at legal risk and can also put you at risk of being fired if things get out of control.

Some companies address inter-office dating in their employee manual. Some even have "love contracts" removing the company from any liability associated with the relationship. So, if you are still tempted to date a coworker check to see if a policy exists addressing the issue.

Someone once told me that she was in a relationship with a man she worked with. He was a great looking guy, an impeccable dresser, and had a great personality – at work. Out of work, he was completely different – a couch potato who spent the weekend in sweats and didn't shower until Monday morning. So, just remember, what you see at work is everyone on their best behavior. For a lot of people, that's as good as it is going to get.

The bottom line is this: Don't sabotage your heart, your job or your career by falling for the temptation to date a coworker. Have good, strong and healthy relationships and romances. Just don't do it in the office.

19

The Office Grapevine

You know it might be a bad day when you go to work the day after the annual office party and people are either avoiding you, high-fiving you, or telling you that what you did last night has already received over 10,000 hits on Youtube.

The office grapevine is an unusual thing. On the one hand it can be a vital, albeit non-official, corporate communication vehicle. On the other hand, it can be a personally damaging medium for rumor, gossip and innuendo.

For some executives, the image of the office rumor-mill is similar to that of the celebrity trash magazines you see at the grocery store check-out lines. And you have to look at it that way too. Yes, in the same way that a broken clock is correct twice a day, sometimes those rags actually do get a story right. But most of the time, they are reporting about teenage aliens mating with Bigfoot on the White House lawn.

So, how should you deal with the grapevine? The best answer is to approach it with great caution and judgment. The office grapevine can provide you with informal communication about events unfolding within the business. That's the good part of the grapevine.

But it can also be where you hear about who is dating who, who is gunning for whose job, and who is having personal problems outside the office. That's the bad part of the grapevine.

You must be able to sift the good information from the bad. But you must also be very aware of how you will be perceived if caught entangled in the grapevine's branches.

Here are some of the things of which to be aware:

- Personal versus business. Is someone telling you something "juicy" about a coworker? If so, STOP listening. Have the integrity to tell the person, "I'm really not interested and don't need to hear about that." Do you know there are very few people with the guts to say that? Most people are more concerned about hurting the gossiper's feelings than they are about the hurt that is being caused by participating in the rumor mill.

- False information and traps. There was a game we used to play when I was a kid called "Telephone." In the game, someone would whisper a phrase into the ear of the kid next to him or her. That kid would then do the same to the next person in line. It would go on until the last person. Finally, the last person would say aloud the phrase that he or she heard. It was often quite different from the original phrase. Office gossip is the same way. You hear about something that was told to you from someone who heard about it from someone else who heard it from someone else and so on. Can you be sure it is accurate? Is someone setting you up to see if you'll spread this information around? If you pass along bad information, you will be branded as not trustworthy. That's not good. If you are hearing information and you cannot verify it as truthful, then drop it like it's hot.

- Personal business information. Is someone telling you how much they make or how much others in the department or company make? Avoid listening because it's none of your business. As far as you are concerned, when you took your position and accepted the salary or pay rate, you made a deal. Finding out how much more someone else makes can only lead to animosity or other bad feelings. A deal is a deal and you should stick to it.

- Confidentiality. During World War II, the saying was "loose lips sink ships." Confidentially was truly a matter of life and death. Can you be trusted with sensitive information? If your manager comes to you in confidence with some type of future plans for the organization, or for you personally, can she trust you to keep it private?

- Be honest with yourself. If you know you are as good at keeping confidential information as a fishing net is with holding water, then don't participate in the rumor mill. If by chance you do happen to come across some interesting tidbit, take it home and tell a friend or family member. Get it out of your system before you risk your own reputation at work.

Simply refuse to become the subject of the office grapevine. Try to live your life without giving anyone a reason to make you a part of the rumor mill. That means no getting sloppy with another coworker at the office picnic, no getting plastered and doing crazy pole dancing at the Friday night happy hour, and, well, you get the picture. It also means no bitching about the boss to other coworkers. The chances are it will get around and you will quickly kiss away any chance to move up the ladder in that company.

Stay away from any conversation that starts out with "Don't tell anyone about this, but…" The chances are you're not the only one who has heard about this. Face it: some people just can't keep a secret. But also know when you're being played. Believe it or not, there are some people who will drop information on you just to see what you know or what other gossip you can offer up. Once you've done that, you're compromised. Just like trying to get toothpaste back in the tube, you can't pull those words back into your mouth.

Also, don't use the office gossip mill to get even with someone. If you have been offended, there are other means available to deal with the problem. Starting rumors or using the grapevine to get your side of the story out there is just not what a mature professional does.

So, err on the side of extreme caution when dealing with the pickings of the office grapevine. Otherwise you risk your managers and coworkers looking at you in the same way they look at the National Enquirer, and I don't think anyone wants to be looked at like that.

20

Politics as Usual

One of corporate life's eternal questions may likely be "How did that idiot get that great job?" Well, the answer to that burning question may just be answered by the term "Office Politics."

If you've never heard the term "Office Politics" before, get ready. You may never hear the actual term used within the confines of the workplace, but if you are interested in advancing your position within your company, you are going to have to understand the concept of office politics and know how the game is played.

Office politics at its essence is the way people use the power, authority, or relationships they have within the organization to influence others and gain advantages beyond their actual role or power.

An example that illustrates this is in the area of manager-subordinate relationships. Let's say there is a manager who is managing six people in her department. One of those she manages shares her passion for marathon running. The subordinate just happens to get herself invited to some training runs with the manager. Over time they develop a friendly relationship that would not have happened during the confines of the normal business routine. While performing their long training runs, they discuss many things, including the dynamics at the office. During these conversations, the manager is able to get valuable information from the employee about what is really going on with the other people on the team. At the same time, the subordinate is putting herself in a great position of confidence and trustworthiness with the manager.

Back in the office, the employee is now able to go into the manager's office at any time, close the door and influence the manager's decision making process in a way the others could not. When that employee is promoted to fill a recently opened supervisor's position, nobody is really surprised. Office politics has just happened.

Office Politics differs from the Office Grapevine in that those involved in politics are usually looking for an ability to gain an advantage in certain situations. The grapevine is often about trying to use the rumor mill as a means of socializing, without necessarily trying to attain personal advancement. Though they have many of the same elements, they are used to achieve different ends.

Office politics is often how average workers close the gap on their more skilled peers when competing for upward mobility. Sometimes, witnessing office politics can be painful and embarrassing to watch. It can be filled with "brown-nosers" and "yes-men" trying to do or say anything to ingratiate themselves with their managers. If you actually have any sense of personal integrity, you may find yourself needing to take a really hot shower after witnessing a true suck-up at work.

To be sure, office politics can get pretty ugly and, at times, even vicious if one person has it out for another. Office politics can often be perceived as people doing whatever they can for themselves regardless of the carnage or bad-blood they leave in their wake. Based on that, a lot of people feel they just don't want to be a player in the office politics game. The truth of the matter though is that in order to advance in the workplace, you must play the game.

But, I have good news for you. You can actually practice office politics without swallowing your pride or trashing your honor. I actually like to call it Office Positioning versus Office Politicking. Here is how to successfully position yourself within your organization without feeling like you've just sold out to Satan.

- Solicit advice from your manager. Take a problem that you are dealing with, develop several options, and determine the one you think is the best alternative. Then go to your manager and ask him to help provide guidance on your thought process. This lets him know two things. First, you value his opinion and look at him as an expert. Making a manager feel like an expert in him field will be a huge ego stroke for him. That's good for you. Second, it is a good way to demonstrate your logic process and ability to communicate. Pretty soon the manager will feel that you are also becoming an expert with good communication skills and that puts you in line for managing others.
- Make sure you are communicating your successes to your management. Once you get a task done, be sure they know about it. It is not bragging to let people know you are someone who can get the job done. Developing a reputation as one who gets results will earn you the respect of your management.
- Take on challenging or undesirable tasks that others may not have time to do. This shows your desire and ability to go above and beyond your "job description." It also shows you have self-confidence and are interested in broadening your experience with the company. During the activity, send out a periodic note to your management looking for feedback or to review your draft findings and/or conclusions. When you've completed the task, make sure you fully communicate your results to your management.
- Develop professional relationships beyond your own department. The more people you know, the better are your opportunities for advancement within the company. Also, if there is ever a time when your department ends up on the corporate chopping block, it will be helpful to have allies in other parts of the company that may be able to help keep you aboard.
- Volunteer to help your peers when they are swamped with an

overload of work or an upcoming deadline. Be sure to let your management know that you are available to help others out even though it may mean you will need to work extra hours to do so.

- Be sure your skills are closely aligned with the direction your company is heading. For instance, being an expert at an obsolete technology or methodology that your company is replacing will not help you get ahead. Find out where your company is going, learn what you can about it, then find a way to demonstrate that knowledge to your management.

No matter how rough the politics get in your office, as stated in other parts of this book, always remember the Golden Rule. Treat others as you would want them to treat you. If you respect others, regardless of their position or rank within the organization, you will earn an equal amount of respect. The Golden Rule is described in more detail in the Quick Hits section of this book.

Gaining the respect of others through your actions and deeds, while not sacrificing your own core values, will help you win at the game of office politics.

21

What's Your Name Again?

Comedian Jerry Seinfeld includes a very funny bit in his act about remembering names. He describes the most uncomfortable of moments when someone whose name he's forgotten approaches him with a big, "Hi Jerry!" and all he can come up with is "Oh, Hello, You." It's really funny, really true, and really awkward.

During your first year, and most likely for the rest of your career, you will be meeting many new contacts. People are usually impressed and feel special when you remember their names. Remembering names helps you establish rapport with people. These days, when many companies put a premium on one's interpersonal skills and abilities, being able to do those little things, like remembering someone's name, will set you apart from the pack.

By the same token, if you persistently forget someone's name and use the Jerry Seinfeld method, you run the risk of making them feel unimportant to you.

So, how do you develop the habit of remembering people's names? There are several different techniques that professionals use to gain this most valuable skill.

First, pay attention. Most of us when first meeting someone are so caught up in what we're going to say or our own image, we totally ignore the introduction. So, when introduced to someone else, actually pay attention to the introduction.

Then, once you've been introduced, you need to remember the name. So, repeat it. Repeat it in your mind, and then repeat it to the person. You should immediately say something like, "Nice to meet you, John." Within a minute or two, try to use the name again. You might say something like, "So, John, how long have you worked here." When leaving the person, be sure to use the name again by saying, "John, it was good to meet you." You may also want to ask for a business card at this point.

When you have the chance to do so, write the name down in a contact file. I actually keep a notebook simply with names of people I meet. It's a pretty simple method. After I meet someone, I enter their name in my cell phone. Then when I get back to my desk I write it down, along with some other information about that person, including where and when we met, and any other pertinent information.

You can synch your phone with your email system or enter the new contact information into a spreadsheet or a database or whatever. For me, the contact notebook seems to work. Whenever I go to a conference or another gathering where I may run into some of the folks I've met earlier, I review the notebook to refresh my memory.

Some people try to remember names by using gimmicks like word association. That technique suggests doing things like making a mental connection between the person's name and something more familiar. So, if you meet someone named Charlie, you would think of Charlie Brown, or if you meet someone named Sarah, you would think of Sarah Lee.

Other suggested methods include mentally picturing people's names written on their foreheads. So, not only do you hear the name, but then you visualize it, too.

If you are in a situation where none of these techniques work for you, you can just be candid and direct. If after an initial introduction you can not remember a person's name, be honest and ask him or her to repeat it. Most people are happy to oblige and will take it that you really care and want to remember their name.

Since many people are "bad with names," they may find your honesty in asking again an admirable thing. However, if after two times you still can not remember, use other means.

You may ask for a business card like this: "Say, last time we met, I meant to get a business card. Would you happen to have one now?" You may ask a mutual friend, "I just had a very interesting conversation with a colleague of yours from your finance department and I forgot her name..."

Hopefully, with these techniques, you will never have to go through life worrying about coming face-to-face with "what's his name," or the Seinfeldian, "Oh, Hello You."

22

R-E-S-P-E-C-T – That's What Success Means To Me

I referenced the Golden Rule earlier in the book and go into a bit more detail in a later chapter. It's actually a paraphrase of a Biblical concept and it goes something like "treat others as you would have them treat you."

On the other end of the philosophical spectrum is German philosopher Immanuel Kant who said, "Act in such a way that you always treat humanity, whether in your own person or in the person of any other, never simply as a means, but always at the same time as an end."

Even my own mother, a philosopher in her own right, used to always tell me to "respect my elders."

So, the idea of respecting those around you is one that spans ideologies. Since the workplace is an area where you will be surrounded with many new people, it is a place where the practice of respecting others is vital. Remember there is no guarantee that people will automatically show you respect. For a lot of people, especially those in positions higher up the corporate ladder, respect will be something you will need to earn.

So, respect in the workplace is at least two-dimensional. That is, you show respect to others and you work to gain respect from others.

Showing respect to others in the workplace should be an easy thing for most people to do, but once you've been in the workplace for a few months, you'll realize how many people just don't get it. In fact, a good synopsis of this book could be that it teaches you how to give and get respect in the workplace. So, learning and practicing the concepts in these pages should help you attain the respect of your managers and coworkers.

But, since we are specifically talking about arming you with techniques, tips and tricks, here are just a few displays of how people do not show respect in the work place. Just make sure NONE of these resemble you.

- Loud and/or obnoxious telephone ringers.
- Taking the last cup of coffee and not making another pot.
- Not saying thank you, please, etc.
- Not refilling the copier machine paper bin even though the machine is flashing a sign at you, yes you, to refill the paper tray.
- Any release of bodily gasses, or its cousin, bad-breath (one word: MINTS).
- Really smelly lunches that may have been a delicacy in the old country, but may cause those within a 10 yard radius to gag violently.
- Lurking around someone while they're on the phone and trying to peak at what's on their computer screen.
- Telling inappropriate jokes, using profanity, bragging about personal escapades, or generally just gossiping about others.
- Clogging up coworkers' in-boxes with non-work-related emails.
- Talking really loudly, which is closely related to laughing really loudly, which is a distant relative of playing your music really loudly.
- Having a really messy workspace that becomes a distraction to

those around you.

Of course, the list on how to show disrespect to others could go on, but you get the idea. Don't be that guy or girl who is considered rude and disrespectful through these kinds of actions.

So, how do you earn respect? That's an easy one too. But it requires hard work. Well, actually, that's basically it. Be a hard worker. In addition:

- Be dependable – when you say you're going to do something, just do it.
- Be agreeable with your manager and with those around you.
- Be a volunteer for undesirable tasks and assignments.
- Be kind to those who help you and even those who don't.
- Be thoughtful when answering questions or approaching a tough assignment; don't just blurt out an answer to try to impress.
- Take ownership and responsibility for your actions, especially if things go wrong.
- Don't blame others for your mistakes.
- Make it your job to make your boss successful.
- Don't be a sell-out on your principles. That is if you are not a liar, don't lie. If you're not a cheater, don't cheat. If you're not a thief, don't steal.
- Show deference to those who have been with the company longer than have you. They probably do know more than you, believe it or not.

Remember a few other things about earning and giving respect. Respect is about valuing the humanness of others. Respect means that you treat others with dignity; that is you don't beat someone when they're down, you don't embarrass someone in front of others, and you don't criticize someone excessively for poor performance. The workplace is truly a great melting pot where people of all ages, races, nationalities, beliefs and lifestyles come together to meet a greater goal. So, gaining respect of others most certainly means you never prejudge someone based on their race, religion, gender or any other non-relevant personal characteristic.

With respect to respect, the bottom line is this: A professional does not move up the corporate ladder by climbing over the backs of others. Treat all those around you with dignity and decency and they will carry you to the top.

23

Minding Your Manners

If your mother was anything like mine, I'm sure you have heard about the importance of having good manners. Of course, my mother was mostly concerned about me saying "please," "thank you" and holding the door open for other people. But had she thought about it, I'm sure she would have also had a lot to say about having good manners on the job.

In the workplace, good manners will not necessarily be noticed or pointed out. But you can be sure bad manners will be. Practicing good manners will usually add to the good impression people are already forming about you. Bad manners may be called out, may show up on performance reviews, and will definitely impact your promotional options.

Bad manners are always noticed and will have an immediate and important impact on your reputation. They may also have an influence on the opportunities presented to you by your management. If you are perceived as having poor manners, there may be doubt as to whether you can represent your company in a respectable and dignified manner.

For instance, most employers will not feel comfortable sending someone who is known to have poor table manners to take a client out to a business lunch or dinner. In the same way, one who lacks telephone etiquette will not be asked to call an important customer.

According to an October, 2004 survey by The Creative Group, forty percent of executives believe the level of courteousness in the workplace is significantly worse than it was in the mid-1990s. So, what this means to you is opportunity. As a new professional, if the trend is toward more boorish behavior among your peers, you will stand out by practicing good manners and etiquette.

Some of the in-office etiquette blunders to avoid include:

- Non-productive noises from your cubicle. These might include drumming with your pencil, overuse of your speakerphone, playing music or listening to the radio without headphones, etc.
- Foul language of any kind.
- Interrupting coworkers without letting them complete their comments. Also, interrupting coworkers while they are talking on the phone.
- Inappropriate use of email or instant messaging.
- Using improper grammar and slang. For instance, to answer someone in the affirmative, use the word "Yes" instead of "Yeah" or "Uh-huh."
- Being late to meetings or running your meetings beyond the planned completion time.
- Not keeping your work area clean. Not cleaning up after yourself in the kitchen, break-room or bathroom.

My mother was also a stickler for table manners. One of the biggest impression killers will be to go out for a meal with a group of your coworkers or managers and start eating like a pig. Here are a few tips to remember when it comes to dining out with your business colleagues or clients.

- Use the fork and knife rule when you order. Sandwiches and finger foods can be messy and will leave you with dirty hands that your client may be reluctant to shake after your meal is complete.

- Leave the finger-licking for the fried chicken fast food place. Do not ever lick your fingers during a business meal.

- Don't start eating until at least all have been served.

- Smoking or drinking alcohol during business meals is generally unacceptable. Avoid these behaviors.

- Unless you're with a few close co-workers, do not ask for doggy bags.

- Practice good posture by sitting up straight at the table. It will give you a professional, authoritative and confident appearance.

- Nobody wants to see the food in your mouth. Do not chew with your mouth open or talk with your mouth full.

- Do not slurp the soup from your bowl or the drink from your straw.

- Do not spit a piece of bad food back onto your plate. Instead, bring your napkin to your mouth, put the food in the napkin, then fold it and return it to your lap. If necessary, request a new napkin from your server.

The thoughts and tips in this chapter are just the tip of the iceberg when it comes to the importance of etiquette in the workplace. If you have any doubt about your knowledge or ability in this area, you should do a bit more research. There are many resources from websites, books and even etiquette classes that you can take to round out your skills.

Practicing good manners in the workplace sounds like a given. But you would be surprised at how many people don't use them. Proper etiquette and manners is a finishing touch to your overall professional image.

As previously mentioned, people won't give you an award for the way you hold a fork or for properly thanking someone for a deed well-done. But when you are well-mannered, the impression you leave with your management will tell them you are a professional and are ready for the next move up the corporate ladder.

24

Management Support

One of the best ways to get ahead in the business world is to do everything you can to make your boss successful. Face it, your manager is already proven in your company's eyes. He or she already has upward mobility. If you work hard to make your manager successful, your manager may get moved up. If you have played your cards right, when your boss gets promoted, you may get pulled right along.

You can learn to support your boss in a number of ways and none of them require you to be a suck-up. When you support your manager, you enhance your value to your company. When you support your manager, you will be considered loyal and trustworthy. When you support your manager, you will likely be rewarded either through promotion, raises or other opportunities.

The first way to support your manager is to get behind their decisions. This is not to say that your boss needs a "yes-person." In fact, most managers see through those who just agree with them in order to avoid conflict or to ingratiate themselves. What most managers want on their teams are people who can bring different ideas, valid options and solid opinions to achieve organizational goals. But once the manager makes a decision, there should be no second guessing or "I told you so" from the team. There is a time to debate and a time to salute.

Good managers appreciate vigorous debate, then absolute support once the debate is over. Even if your idea or project is rejected, support the decision. Use the same creativity you used to develop your idea by implementing the management decision.

Do not bad mouth the decision or the project. Do not express anger or disappointment with the decision maker regardless of whom you are speaking with. And you do not need to discard your idea or work; it may be valuable in the future.

At this point in your career, you have not been exposed enough to learn all of the reasons why decisions are made. Some may seem political, some may not make sense. In the arena of ideas, you're going to win a few and you're going to lose a few. It is not important that all of your ideas are accepted. What is important is how you respond once a decision is made. It is most important for you to be considered a team player by your peers and by those for whom you work.

Don't take this to mean that you should not express opinions or put your ideas out there; however, once the decision is made be a team player and support your manager.

Another way to show support for your manager is to respect his or her position in the organization chart. It is not appropriate to ignore the chain of command by going over your manager's head to get your idea heard. Again, your boss' boss needs to have trust in the organization structure and in those who are running the company. Trust me that if your manager finds out you've been going behind his or her back feeding information up the chain, you will be put in a very uncomfortable position and your chances of advancement will be much more diminished.

By the way, if there are issues about which you feel uncomfortable speaking with your manager, such as harassment or other personnel type issues, you should always feel free to communicate directly with your human resources department representative.

Dependability is another way to support your manager. Show up to work when you are supposed to be there. Don't use up sick days unless you're really sick. Don't schedule vacation time during critical work periods. Just being at work is a great support of your manager. As an old boss of mine used to tell me, "Your best ability is your dependability."

Being a positive force on your team is also another way to support your manager. All good managers appreciate constructive feedback, even if it is negative. However, if you are constantly going into your manager's office talking about all the things that are wrong with your peers, your department, your project, the company, etc., you'll soon be an unwelcome guest.

Managers actually like hearing encouraging feedback. Share your successes and be sure to share praises for the achievements of others on the team. By doing this, your manager knows that you are confident and not threatened by the success of others. Again, that is a sign of maturity that will set you apart from the others.

Finally, a great way to support your manager is to seek his or her feedback on your performance. A good manager will from time-to-time offer constructive advice about how well you are doing in your job. If your company does not have a formal review process, ask him or her for a performance review. Seek out areas in your work that could use improvement and ask for clarity in understanding areas where you may be falling short of expectations.

Ask about patterns in your work performance that your manager may see, but you don't. Ask for any additional skills or training you may need to help you better perform your duties. Once you request feedback, then accept it, both positive and negative. Remember, don't personalize any negative feedback. If you have an honest manager, then participating in this process will only make you a better, more valuable employee.

Remember, your ticket to future advancement may be tied to your manager's success. Make your manager successful and enjoy the ride.

25

Here's Lookin' At Ya – Sexual Harassment

While this book is not meant to offer legal advice, there is one area that you need to know about that if not approached correctly could lead you, your career, and maybe even your company, into big trouble. That is the area of sexual harassment.

Look, just like in most colleges, the workplace is one where both men and women interact very closely with each other. There are long days and business trips and social activities and all kinds of coed activities in the business world. Needless to say, the condition of having young men and women spending eight or more hours, five days a week in very close proximity, and sharing a common challenging work experience, may be an equation for some serious personal feelings to develop. The difference is that in the area of romantic interactions, cross-gender or otherwise, what may have been acceptable, or should I say what you could get away with, in college, may not at all be tolerable in the workplace.

Harassment of any kind in the workplace may be considered illegal, but this chapter will just be a quick look at harassment of the sexual kind. It is by no means a substitution for a human resources or legal policy guide. Most companies offer some type of sexual harassment training, so by all means take advantage of that and follow whatever the company suggests in this area.

So what is sexual harassment? There are actually two different definitions. One is what is called quid pro quo. That is loosely translated from Latin for "you do something for me, I'll do something for you." So, in the sexual harassment area, it may mean a boss says you sleep with me and I'll give you the raise, promotion, etc. The second type of sexual harassment is often defined as "unwelcome verbal, visual, or physical conduct of a sexual nature that is severe or pervasive and affects working conditions or creates a hostile work environment."

I don't want to second guess or undermine anything that your company is telling you in their own training in this area. But I do want you to know that everyone perceives things differently. You may think the little jokes you told or emails you sent were just harmless and cute. Someone else may have found them unwanted and offensive. You may think you are complementing someone by commenting on their clothes or looks. Someone else may think you are making unwanted sexual advances.

Perceptions are so different from person to person that it is absolutely necessary for you to be aware of the many areas where behaviors may be interpreted as harassment. In fact, offenses can occur, not only verbally, but also visually and physically. Following are some examples of what might be considered sexual harassment. While it is not an exhaustive list, it gives you an idea or what sexual harassment may be considered to be.

Visual: These are things of yours that people can easily see. They include pictures, screensavers, etc. that are of a sexual matter.

Verbal or Written: These are things you say or send. They include comments you make, or letters, notes, e-mails, texts, or instant messages you send addressing a person's clothing or body, sex-based jokes, requests for sexual favors or repeated request for a date. They also include spreading rumors about a person's sex life.

Nonverbal: These are body language types of communications, which include checking out a person by looking up and down at his or her body, inappropriately staring at a certain part of a person's body, or making derogatory gestures a sexual nature. Also, respect a person's personal space. Some people stand so close to others that it can make for very awkward and uncomfortable situations. Try to be at least arm's length from others to keep it safe.

Physical: These are any physical touching of a person's body or clothing. It includes kissing, hugging or stroking. Keep your hands to yourself. If you're the touchy-feely type, resist the temptation to reach out and touch someone. You will be putting yourself and your company at risk. I'm not kidding; some people are looking for any reason to sue their company to get that big pay-off.

Also, remember that just because something is not reported immediately, it does not mean you are off the hook for harassing someone. During sexual harassment trials or investigations, evidence is presented years after the fact. Remember, texts, IMs, emails, etc. can be stored for years and may come back to haunt you.

Beyond just the legal impacts of sexual harassment, there are career consequences for everyone involved in these types of incidents. If you are a consistent harasser, you will be perceived as a boorish thug with a high creep factor and you will not have a chance to excel within your company. No right-minded business will promote someone who has the chance to put the company at legal risk. They will no more advance a sexual harasser to a position of authority of other people than they would promote an embezzler to watch over the cash register.

For the sake of your reputation and your career, you need to be extremely cautious in the way you communicate with your fellow employees. Remember, you are in the workplace to work. You are

there to conduct business. All of your communications, whether
verbal or otherwise, are subject to interpretation. Don't let an off-
the-cuff comment derail what could be a great career. Be professional
in all that you do and make sure you are always sending out the right
message.

Part 3

Rookie Psychology

26

Why Everyone Loves Puppies

Do you know why people love puppies? I think it's because puppies are always happy to see you. They don't care about your past. They don't care about what you look like. They don't care about how much money you have or what kind of car you drive or how nice your apartment is. They are just always happy to see you.

While it's impossible to have everyone in the world like you, it is possible to have an attitude that makes you the type of person that people like to be around. Not only that, but next to your ability, your attitude will be one of the most important factors contributing to whether or not promotions come your way.

Aside from good performance and potential, those with happy, friendly attitudes who treat people around them with respect are often the ones who will be selected for promotions. I know it's not scientific, but in the Donald Trump TV show, "The Apprentice", it always seemed that most people wanted the jerk fired…and it usually turned out that way.

You've maybe even seen it in school. Two people got in trouble for the same thing. The one with the reputation for being arrogant and cocky usually got into more trouble than the one who was thought of as being a nice friendly person.

The great thing about attitude is it is truly the one thing you can control. Unfortunately, too many people allow their attitude and moods to be controlled by others. Rev. Chuck Swindoll may have said it best:

> "The longer I live, the more I realize the impact of attitude on life. Attitude to me is more important than facts. It is more important than the past, than education, than money, than circumstances, than failures, than success, than what other people think, say or do. It is more important than appearance, gift, or skill. It will make or break a company...a church...a home.
>
> The remarkable thing is we have a choice every day regarding the attitude we will embrace for that day. We cannot change our past... The only thing we can do is play on the string we have, and that is our attitude.
>
> I am convinced that life is 10% what happens to me and 90% how I react to it. And so it is with you... we are in charge of our attitudes. ... Attitude keeps me going or cripples my progress. It alone fuels my fire or assaults my hope. When my attitudes are right, there is no barrier too high, no valley too deep, no dream too extreme, no challenge too great for me." – Rev. Chuck Swindoll

Of course, it is always easy to have a positive attitude to nice people. The challenge comes in being nice to the more difficult ones you work with. But there is a pay-off even in that. I have a friend named Jeff who told me one of the reasons he was promoted to team supervisor was specifically because his management saw how he was able to deal positively with even the biggest jerk on the team. When Jeff became the supervisor, the guy was still a jerk, but since Jeff had always engaged him, listened to his ideas and treated him with respect, he always gave Jeff his strongest support.

Having a friendly attitude towards those you work with will help you in the future if you need someone to cover your back or help you out during a challenging time. You may also want to consider how you would be perceived when a future employer calls your company looking for a reference.

Being kind and respectful to people goes beyond those on your team and your management. You should also be friendly to the company support staff. That could mean the administrative assistants, the clerical staff, the mailroom help, even the janitorial and maintenance crews.

Every person has dignity and nobody is beneath you in human worth. You don't need to become best friends with everyone, but you should never condescend toward lower level employees based on their position. Their positions are important to the operation of your business and believe it or not, they may end up being important allies to you in the future. Just remember the old adage, "You'd better be nice to the people you meet on your way up the corporate ladder, because you may need their support on the way back down."

Having a good attitude and a positive temperament goes beyond the way you treat people. It also includes the way you react to the ever-present change that occurs in the workplace. There are so many things within your company that are now outside of your control. There are policy changes, promotions, hirings and firings, ideas about how to market a product, and a gazillion other decisions within the workplace that may not make sense to you. You may even disagree strongly with them.

In fact, you may have a bunch of people with whom you work that don't agree with certain management decisions. But after a while, if you are the one always involved in pointing out what's wrong, you'll be labeled as a whiner or a complainer. Eventually, people will get bored with your act and will prejudge any of your other contributions.

On the other hand, the person who understands that change is a constant in the workplace has a better time adapting to the change and can actually take advantage of the opportunity it may present. When your management sees you being a champion for supporting their decisions, as opposed to being pulled along kicking and screaming, you will be set apart as a candidate for future promotion.

It's all about your attitude. You can choose to be nice to people who are not very nice. You can choose to accept change that may require more work for you to adapt. You can choose to accept the new product line or marketing approach. Or not.

It is a guarantee that change will happen in your life. It is a guarantee that you will have to work with difficult people. It is a guarantee that life will give you ups and downs, successes and failures. Fortunately, it's a guarantee that you can control the way you respond. One way will lead you to wallow in the quicksand and hardly ever move forward. The other way will lead you to much success throughout your entire life.

27

Procrastination – You Can Pain Me Now or You Can Pain Me Later

I have always thought the most important minute is the last minute. It seems to be the singular moment where nearly everything gets done. Things hardly ever get done in the first or second minute... they always seem to wait for that ever so popular last minute. Why do you think that is?

Procrastination is the answer. If you just left college, you probably witnessed or maybe even practiced procrastination yourself. Maybe you were assigned a relatively simple project and had all semester to get it done, but you waited until two weeks before the due date to start working on it.

It makes sense. When you've been given 2 months to complete a simple task, it seems like plenty of time. So, you put off getting started in order to work on other things that seemed to have a more immediate priority. Then the due date for the project is right around the corner and, all of a sudden, that real easy project got real hard real fast.

Benjamin Franklin, one of our nation's Founding Fathers, once said, "You may delay, but time will not." In well run businesses, time is of the essence. Things are planned out, scheduled and executed. When people don't follow through on their part of the plan, the system starts breaking down. The company misses opportunities to make more revenue or to save on expenses. Most companies will not keep people around who cause them to miss those types of opportunities.

At the heart of delayed or missed opportunities has to be procrastination. Somebody put off doing something until it was too late, then the dominoes started falling.

So, why do people procrastinate? Have you ever thought about that? Tony Robbins, a renowned motivational trainer, believes that procrastination is all about perceptions of pain and pleasure. He says that those who procrastinate often link more perceived pain in performing a task now versus not taking any action at all. In other words, we think it will be too difficult to take action now, so we put it off thinking there will be less difficulty taking action later. Unfortunately, putting off the task often results in more actual pain later.

For instance, let's say you have to call a customer to request more information for an important loan application. You have already collected a mountain of paperwork and know the customer is going to be unpleasant when you make the request. So, you perceive the call will be somewhat painful. But, by putting off this phone call, you may be creating a much more painful situation by delaying this request – the loan approval might be delayed or, worse, declined. Believe me, you will then have a lot more pain to deal with in that case.

So, in addition to Tony Robbins' pain/pleasure principle, what are other reasons for procrastination?

- You are a perfectionist. You feel that if you can't do the task perfectly, it is nearly impossible to start.

- You're a dreamer. You spend a lot of time thinking and telling others about how great things will be once the project is complete, but always have difficulty taking action on your great idea.

- You're an over-committer. You say yes to every request made of you because you don't want to displease those in your life. Then you can't get things done on time complaining you have too much to do.

- You love chaos. You are the kind of person who loves the adrenaline rush associated with getting things done just before the deadline.

No matter what the reason for procrastinating, you must find a way to overcome this habit. Although the Internet is filled with resources for dealing with procrastination, here are a few tips:

1. Identify the actions that you are delaying. Write them down in a list. This helps you to see the magnitude of what you need to do.
2. Next to each item list the reasons for putting them off. Be honest about your reasons: fear, feeling overwhelmed, not a priority, etc.
3. Now list next to each of those items the cost of delay. Think about the impact on those who are depending on you getting the task done. Think about the reaction from your manager or others on your team by not getting them done.
4. Next, list the first three things that need to be done to get the task started or completed. Include a realistic estimate for how long each of those sub-tasks will take to complete.
5. Finally, put dates and times next to each of those sub-tasks. Actually make a timeline or schedule for when you will be able to work on those tasks.

Hopefully, this plan will help you get things started – and completed.

Procrastination can make your job harder than it already may be. It can kill your chance for advancement within your organization. Businesses want to promote people who get things done. They want doers, not talkers. Procrastination may be the biggest reason why bright people never reach their fullest potential.

The best time to start working on anything is today, because tomorrow is already full.

28

When Tempers Flare

When you join the professional ranks, you will be amazed at some of the crazy decisions and activities that go on. Sometimes, those decisions impact you, and not in a good way. Someone may screw up on a commitment and your boss decides everyone needs to work this Saturday to fix the problem. Or, a vendor could blow a critical order and cause you to delay a shipment to one of your customers. Or, maybe, you just lost a best-commission-of-my-life sale to a competitor. If you like your weekends, don't like missing your deadlines, or needed that sale to make your monthly quota, then you may be justifiably angry.

There is nothing wrong with anger. It's just another emotion. You are entitled to be angry about things that, well, anger you. Just like you are able to be happy, sad, frustrated, or joyful. The thing you have to remember is that anger generally, if acted out inappropriately, has the potential to have you labeled as hot-headed or foolish.

Remember, a point of this book is to give you tools and techniques to deal with the inevitable calamities of the workplace. So, if you know you are prone to impulsively act on your anger, you need a strategy to deal with it. Bear in mind, being angry is not going to get you in trouble. Punching a hole in the wall, kicking a chair or screaming at one of your co-workers will.

Everyone is human and prone to make a mistake now and then. Even you. Face it, some workplaces are Petri dishes for blunders. It's just going to happen. But people are people. Yelling at them may feel good for the moment. It may even get you the results you were looking for. But getting angry and blowing up usually works against you in the long run. You may lose an important ally or a supplier if you blow up and hurt someone's feelings or cause them embarrassment.

The first thing you need to be able to do is recognize when you are getting angry. I know that sounds like a big "duh," but usually the signs of an impending blow-up are there ahead of time. Different people feel anger in different ways. But before your brain tells you to launch into a verbal punch in the nose on your boss or co-worker, there are other signs. You might start breathing faster, feel your heart beat racing, or feel your muscles start to tense. You might start turning bright red or feel a certain flush coming over you.

Once you start feeling the signs of anger, there are some things you can do to diffuse the condition. First of all, if it is at all possible, take a walk. Walk outside, walk down the hall, walk to the water-fountain. Just try to remove yourself from the situation. Now, you may be in a place or meeting where you can not just up and walk away. If that is the case, then do what your mom always told you to do. Count to 10 and breathe deeply. You would be surprised at how well a few deep breathes before opening your mouth will help you to keep your composure. Once you are able to excuse yourself from the people you are with, then take that walk. Then breathe. Then try to get clear thoughts about what just happened.

Finally, once the dust has settled and you feel you are in the right frame of mind, document the event. This should be done while it is still fresh in your memory if possible. This is a good idea especially if the issue may be raised again in the future. Something can always go wrong when you are trying to get something done in the workplace. Learning from history can help prevent them happening again in the future.

Documenting those things that put you in an angry state of mind not only lets you work through the situations, but it also builds a "lessons learned" file that will be invaluable knowledge for future activities. What should you write about? Here's a list for starters:

- What was the cause of the situation?
- What was my role in the event?
- How can this be avoided in the future?
- What can I learn from this?

You will likely find going through this journaling process will not only give you a sense of calm, but you will also find insights about the situation you would possibly never realize.

No matter how angry you get, do not lash out via email or telephone until you can calm down and get your thoughts together. Even then, if you feel you need to write an email to someone, feel free to draft it, but don't send it until you've had a chance to sleep on it. A word said in anger will most often lead you to have to apologize to someone, no matter who was at fault.

As you consider those things that cause you to become angry, you may also notice a pattern that has its root cause in having a generally stressful life. High levels of stress may cause your anger trigger to be a bit more sensitive.

Believe it or not, anger in the work place may actually work for some people. You will find somewhere on your career path that you'll run into some supervisors who get their way by throwing tantrums and screaming at everyone as if all the world is out to ruin their day. You will wonder how those idiots ever got their jobs. Usually, it is a sign of a poor management culture within the organization. Some companies do actually think that someone who uses anger to get things done is a valuable driving force in the organization. But do not feel compelled to use that type of behavior as your own model.

If you took a show of hands, most people would not want to have anything to do with that person. The yellers and desk pounders may use fear and bullying to advance their own careers, but they will probably die from a heart attack long before they cash their first pension check. Trust me, being perpetually angry is not a good way to go through life.

Of course, this is not meant to be a book on psychology, so if you are really dealing with anger issues on a regular basis, it may be a good idea to get some help. Use your employee assistance program, if available. Even talking to a close friend or family member may help put you in control of your anger instead of letting your anger control you and hurt your career.

29

When It's Time To Sink or Swim

It was Chinese philosopher Lao-tzu who once said, "A journey of a thousand miles begins with a single step."

Let's face it. At one point or another we all may develop or experience some feelings of inadequacy or of being overwhelmed. It's that sudden realization that you may have gotten yourself in way over your head. If, and more likely, when it happens to you, realize you're not alone. It happens to everyone from time to time. What it requires from you is to take that first step.

When you get snowed under by a project or a request to do some difficult task, you need to gain perspective. You need to take a deep breath and take a step back to see the big picture of what you are being asked to do.

Also, remember that you are now a professional. You have just completed your degree and have real skills, both learned and natural. You can conquer this project and overcome your feelings by generally following these four rules:

    a) Divide and Conquer
    b) Organize and Prioritize
    c) Delegate and Share
    d) Get to it

Let's look at a common IT example. Say you're an analyst on an IT project team and your new project is to develop a new set of customized screens for a set of users.

Divide and Conquer. This is a term that is often heard in the military and in politics, among other places. The goal of this step is to take the overall project and break it down into smaller chunks, or maybe even phases, of activity.

In this case, dividing and conquering might mean determining the number of user screens required, as well as the purpose of each of those screens. You can even start with the Welcome Screen, if appropriate. Once you have your list of screens, you start to get a feel for how big the scope of the effort is. Now you have divided the project into smaller parts to attack.

Prioritize and Organize. Using this same example, now that you know the number of screens and their purpose, you can start to prioritize them into the proper order and organize them into logical groupings based on their priority. For instance, you can organize the screens that are used for data entry from those that are used to generate reports. Then, you may want to prioritize within those categories based on any number of criteria. For instance, you may want to program the easier ones first. Sometimes getting the more menial tasks completed frees up your mind to focus on the more complex tasks.

Delegate and Share. Once you have you arms around the smaller tasks that need to be performed you may still feel it is more than you can handle on your own. In that case, it is wise for you to work with your manager to delegate some of the work or share it with others on your team. Believe me, your manager will be impressed that you have broken down and organized the work to this point. A good manager would rather share work across a team ahead of time, than find out at the eleventh hour that you are going to miss a deadline.

Get to it. Now that you have your work organized into smaller pieces and you have a proper work load, there's nothing left to do but start the work.

One of the beauties of dividing and conquering is that with every task you complete, you can get a feeling of accomplishment. There is nothing more discouraging than looking down a long dark tunnel and not seeing a glimmer of sunlight. This happens often in the beginning stages of a new project.

So, don't get discouraged and don't agonize over what may at first appear to be an insurmountable task. Instead, break the big pieces into smaller pieces, get organized, and get started.

In no time you will begin completing some of the parts that will make the whole. Before you know it, the puzzle will start to take shape. Then, after a while, you'll look back in the rear view mirror and be amazed, and maybe even exhilarated, with all you've been able to accomplish.

30

Patience, Persistence and The Payoff

Be patient in your new job. One of the biggest mistakes people entering the professional job market can make is to get frustrated and quit before actually fully exploring all the opportunities of the new job. It is true that sometimes the reality of the situation is somewhat different than what was your original perception. You need to properly and objectively evaluate if quitting is your best or only option.

After four years or more of college, everybody is ready to go out and start being productive. But some things take time. You may hear it from your parents or friends and you're going to hear it from me too – make sure that you have given your job enough time to prove itself to you and for you to prove yourself to your job.

Every new job is going to require a certain degree of training before you get "turned loose." Some companies have very formal training programs. The large accounting and manufacturing firms are known for these well-rounded approaches to indoctrinating new employees. Others have no such formal program at all. And the vast majority of others fall somewhere in between. You may get a pile of manuals describing company procedures, company products, organization charts, industry regulations, and then some. You may be asked to attend a seminar or two, or to attend an orientation class. You may get a formal training program like "How to Sell in the New

Millennium." You may get all of these things all wrapped up with "OTJT" – On the Job Training. The point is that every job will have a learning curve associated with it.

And remember, you are also learning a whole new way of living. You may most likely be living on your own for the first time. Try not to confuse problems or concerns associated with the responsibilities of your new lifestyle – like a new community, paying your own bills, loneliness, no vacations, and the like – with your new job. Try to keep the two separate and determine that if you are unhappy in your life that you really understand the reasons for your unhappiness.

Again, this does not mean you should never think about trying to find a new job. But, what happens to many people is they quit one job for another without really understanding why it is they were unhappy to begin with. Then they are right back into a situation where they are as unhappy or even more unhappy than they were before. This is a terrible cycle to go through and can be avoided if you take the time to analyze the pros and cons of your situation and then make a decision based on a clear examination of the facts.

Maybe your unhappiness is because you have come to realize that you can not live away from home and loved ones. Or maybe your unhappiness comes from living too close to home and loved ones. Maybe you thought with all this money you were going to be making you could afford the big ticket apartment and car and an expensive nightlife funded by credit cards. Or maybe you have come to realize that you can not have your summers off any more with a month or so off between semesters and a spring break to go along with it.

If these are really the things that are making your life miserable, they are not necessarily related to your job. And they are not reasons to immediately throw in the towel and quit. Character and integrity are often developed by making it through these types of rough times. If you decide that it is these non-job things making you unhappy, then by all means give yourself more time to adjust to the situation.

Try not to allow these frustrating circumstances be an excuse to quit your job.

Remember that things are never so bad that there is no hope. Be patient. Be persistent. The payoff may be right around the corner.

31

A Question of Ethics

Our society offers us quite the conundrum when it comes to mixed messages. Your parents tell you things, your friends tell you things, your teachers tell you things, and the shows you watch and music you listen to tell you things. If you listen to advertisers, you'd obey your thirst, just do it, and know that what happens in Vegas stays in Vegas.

You are being bombarded with messages about what is the right thing to do and what is the wrong thing to do. The Josephson Institute's 2008 Report Card on the Ethics of American Youth, a survey of nearly 30,000 students in the U.S., revealed some interesting results in the area of interpreting right from wrong. Among its conclusions was the following:

- Thirty percent of those surveyed had stolen from a store, and
- Sixty-four percent had cheated on a test in the past year.

What is most concerning about this survey though was that 93 percent of the students said they were satisfied with their personal ethics, and 77 percent affirmed that "when it comes to doing what is right, I am better than most people I know."

OK, so we don't have to do the math to see that something is seriously wrong with this picture. Despite the survey, I still believe when it comes down to it, everyone knows right from wrong.

I just think that in the pressures of the moment, sometimes people choose to do the wrong thing, despite knowing the difference. I also believe people have witnessed all their lives how others get away with doing bad things, and are sometimes even rewarded with fame and fortune. So it seems reasonable to rationalize their own bad behavior.

In the business world, in your quest for upward mobility, you need to be keenly aware of what it means to do the right thing, to have a strong sense of personal ethics. You may get messages like needing to "look out for number one" or it's a "dog-eat-dog world" out there where "the end justifies the means." If you subscribe to these ideas, then you can justify any type of mistreatment of others, dishonesty, cheating, and theft.

But I strongly suggest you reject those ideas. People who cheat and steal may get away with it in the short run, but when they get caught, they have not only harmed themselves, they've brought harm to their company, their customers, their investors, and even their families.

This is the case with so many recent stories in business. In the past few decades, we've experienced the S&L crisis of the 1980s, the Enron and WorldCom scandals within the past decade, and of course more recently, the banking and mortgage crisis that have wreaked all kinds of havoc to the world's economy. Trillions of dollars wiped out and millions of lives ruined by these unethical pursuits.

I'm not going to get political or judgmental, but suffice it to say many people made many millions of dollars while others provided political protection all because they felt they needed to get theirs while the getting was good.

So how do you define business ethics? Well, to start with there really is no distinction between personal, business or any other kind of ethics. You should not live by a set of rules in your personal life and then live by another set of principles when you walk through your office doors.

Having good ethics and morals is all about making the right decision in any aspect of your life, even when those decisions are difficult; even when those decisions may not benefit you in the short run.

So, naturally then, having good ethics in business means things like don't cheat, don't steal and don't lie. It means if you bill clients for time spent working on their projects, only bill for hours actually worked. Otherwise you would get paid for non-working hours. That is considered stealing.

It means if one of your peers comes to you with a great product idea that she is thinking about, don't you take it to your boss before she gets the chance to. That's cheating. Or maybe that's stealing. Either way, it's unethical. Get your own ideas.

It means you don't tell your manager you're sick and can't come into work, when you're actually planning to go shoe shopping with you friends. That's lying and if you're getting paid sick time, then that's stealing, too.

When it all gets boiled down, a failure in business ethics usually comes down to some type of violation of the Golden Rule. Treat others as you would want them to treat you. Learn it, love it, live it. Especially in business.

Let me tell you about one of the most ethical men I've ever known. He was a very successful banker. One day he told a group of us that the key to his success was to make sure every deal he entered into was a win-win for everyone involved. If he felt that he was unfairly taking advantage of the other party in a deal, he would not do it. He probably walked away from millions of dollars of profits in his lifetime, but he made many more times over that in deals where every party benefited. He also slept very well at night.

The subject of business ethics is so important that many businesses are offering training classes to employees to stress how important honesty and decency are to the workplace. For those who already follow an ethical approach to life, you are in high demand.

So, if you want to succeed in business and in life, if you want to be able to sleep at nights and not worry about your past coming back to haunt you, if you want to move up the corporate ladder the right way, then do the right thing. Be the poster child for strong ethics in your business. Good things will happen to you if you do.

Part 4

Quick Hits

32

Bragging, Boring, Snoring

There's a saying that says, "It ain't bragging if it's true." Well, that may be accurate in some areas of life, but in the workplace, there's a fine line between self-promotion and self-absorption. While you want to be sure you are letting your management know about your accomplishments, you need to be careful you're not pushing people away with endless stories about your personal abilities, exploits and conquests. Nothing bores people more than someone who is always talking about themselves. Start bragging and watch out for the glazed eyes and suppressed yawns of your audience.

Bragging has a close companion. Have you ever heard of "one-upmanship?" That's when one person talks about what they've just bought and then another person "One-ups" them by saying, "Yeah, I just bought one too, but I got the upgraded version." In the workplace, that may be something like Sue saying she just finished the XYZ project and Sam saying, he did too, but he got his done faster/better/with less errors. Get the point? Someone describing something they've done is not an invitation to a competition. Just let it go.

There's nothing wrong with correctly promoting yourself when the time is right. And there's nothing wrong with being humble the rest of the time.

33

Foul Language

It should be obvious, but always avoid using foul language. You know the words I'm talking about. They are the ones that are supposed to make us blush. It doesn't matter what industry you are in or how others talk. If others cuss left and right, that doesn't make it right. Be different. Stand out. Set a trend. Be a leader, not a follower.

Believe it or not, people can get fired or worse for using foul language. In fact, I recently read an article where a lawyer was thrown in jail for contempt of court for dropping the "f-bomb." Foul language may sound good in the movies or on TV, but the workplace is no place for the use of expletives.

Along the same lines, the use of racial slurs is totally unacceptable. One way to get escorted out the door of your company, and maybe even face legal matters, is to refer to people of different nationalities, race, religion, or lifestyles by using slang or other derogatory nicknames. It just doesn't fly in today's business environment.

With today's cross-cultural work environment, a person who uses foul language and classless slurs will be no candidate for team management. It's just not going to happen.

Clean language and respect for all coworkers is the sign of a true professional ready for advancement.

34

Keeping Your Cool

One of the things my father always told me was "no matter what, remain calm." It is one of the most important life principles I know. Think about it…it's easy to remain cool when everything is going your way, but what about when things turn south. How will you react when the pressure is on?

The work place can be an incubator for stressful times. There are deadlines, angry customers, and demanding bosses. Not only that, but budget constraints, changing technology, and new competition add more pressure to the workplace atmosphere.

When people react emotionally to a stressful situation, it often becomes difficult for them to clearly identify and respond appropriately to the problem. In addition, there is a high potential for conflict and for people to miscommunicate.

So, when you are faced with a workplace crisis, avoid knee-jerk reactions. Instead, take a deep breath and try to evaluate the situation. Try to list the facts, even writing them down on a notepad or white board. If appropriate, gather your team to perform this exercise. Then with all the facts in front of you, come up with alternative solutions. Engage your management to review the options and together determine the best course of action. If you display leadership during trying times, maintaining an objective approach to business problems without personalizing or assigning blame, you will absolutely stand out among your peers.

Remaining cool even under the most difficult situations is the sign of a strong leader. Maintaining level-headedness in a stressful situation will display a maturity that may greatly enhance your image with those around you, especially your company's management.

35

Elevator Speeches

You never know when you'll be face-to-face with the company president or another high-level executive. But usually, those moments are fleeting and rare. It might be in the cafeteria line, it may be on the sidewalk waiting for a cab, or it may be in the elevator.

During any of those chance meetings, you must be able to make an immediate positive impression with that executive. If the exec asks you what you do at the company, what will you say? Now is not the time to fumble for words. You need to be prepared. The way to do that is to develop and memorize a few elevator speeches.

The notion of an elevator speech is to be able to convey in about 20 – 30 seconds information about anything. As a new business professional, you should have an elevator speech for at least the following:

- Your job
- Your department
- Your background
- Your training
- Your company
- Your current projects and/or efforts

Let's say you're sharing an elevator to the 10th floor with your company's vice president of marketing. She asks you your name, how you are doing and what your position is with the company. Here's an example of an elevator speech about your job:

"Thank you for asking. I am a data analyst in the client services division. Our role is to study the purchasing trends for all customers who have spent more than $1000 with our company over the past year. My job is to study those trends and make product placement recommendations to the marketing department. The goal is to have at least 40% of existing customers make an additional purchase within a 12-month period."

Don't be caught flat-footed and tongue-tied. Have your elevator speeches ready!

36

Pay Attention

When engaged in conversation or listening to a presentation, maintain good posture, keep your eyes focused on the speaker and don't fidget. Breathe deeply to avoid yawning and appearing bored or distracted. Remember that body language sometimes speaks louder than words. So, if you're in a meeting with your boss and it looks like you're not paying attention, you will definitely be sending out the wrong message.

If you're asked to go to a meeting of any type, bring a notepad and a pen. If it's important, write it down. There have been so many times I have seen people attend meetings having nothing to use to take down notes. I remember during a meeting, when a coworker told our boss he had a great memory and didn't need to write anything down. That infuriated our manager as he felt disrespected and knew some important detail would be missed. The guy may have had a great memory, but never went far in that company.

Also, remember it is easier to pay attention when you are listening and not talking during presentations. You have two ears and one mouth. The ears will work a lot better when the mouth is shut.

37

Mentors

The business world is one of fads. Whether its quality improvement processes, cost reduction efforts, upsizing, or whatever, business executives are always looking for the next big thing that will make the company more profitable. When it comes to personal development though, one of the biggest fads of recent is actually one that's been around for a long time. It's called mentoring.

Mentoring is the term used to describe the process of a more experienced person teaching or guiding an inexperienced person in the ways of the world, the business, life, etc. Terms like apprentice, protégé, and taking someone "under your wing," are often used when describing the mentor-mentee relationship.

Nineteenth-century American politician John Crosby has said, "Mentoring is a brain to pick, an ear to listen, and a push in the right direction." A mentor is someone who has the benefit of hindsight, has been through it all, can give you understanding and teach you how to deal with the new challenges you are facing. It's like what Obe-Wan Kenobi was to Luke Skywalker.

Some companies have formal mentoring programs where young up and comers are paired with more experienced workers or executives in order to groom them for leadership. Many companies believe that mentoring programs actually lead to lower turnover with their new employees. Ask your human resources department if they have a formal mentoring program.

If your company does not offer one, you can establish informal mentoring relationships within your organization. These associations typically get formed on their own during the natural course of the business cycle. Many people believe that those involved in informal mentoring actually achieve better career and salary growth since there exists a genuine interest in the mentee by the mentor. They simply just like and trust each other, whereas in a formal arrangement, natural chemistry between the two just may not exist and the program expectations may not be realistic.

Successful people take advantage of every opportunity available to advance their careers. Developing mentors with those in your company will help you avoid the mistakes that could otherwise delay your progress up the corporate ladder.

38

The Gapless Career

In most cases, it is wise to not quit your job unless you have another one lined up. This will be even more applicable as you progress in your career. Future employers will always question gaps in your resume. A gap between employers tells someone either you were fired unexpectedly or you quit abruptly without a back-up plan. Either of these are red-flags.

Now, I'm not saying to stay in your job if it is not right for you. As discussed in a previous chapter, you should be sure you are not being too hasty. If you've been on your new job for less than a year, you may want to do a little soul searching as to just why you want to leave. Is it because it's difficult? Is it because you're home-sick? Is it because you don't like your coworkers? What is the real reason why you are thinking about leaving?

If you really feel that you've given it your all, if you feel that you have given the job an appropriate chance, and if you feel that you are not happy with where this job or company may take you, then by all means start a job search, but don't just quit. Then be discreet in your search. Don't brag to other employees as that information will likely reach your management team.

Find something useful about this job. Remember that while there may be bad times in life, there are hardly bad experiences. You may not have enjoyed the work, the people or something else, but you can still use this experience to learn about yourself and to determine what you do and do not want to get out of your next job and out of your career.

The point to remember here is that if you do decide to leave your current job, be sure you have another one to go right into. Don't create employment gaps in your career that will need to be explained later.

39

Personal Finances – Money, Credit Cards and No Homework

It's the perfect storm. You've got a new job with more money than you've ever made before in your life, a mailbox full of credit card offers and no homework to occupy your evenings and weekends. It has all the makings of a party and shop-till-you drop lifestyle. After all, you've just gone from flipping burgers for minimum wage to cashing in on a $40,000 a year salary. But, it also has all the ingredients for a lifestyle trap that may take years to dig out of.

It may start out slowly. A new pair of $200 shoes. A new Nintendo Wii. A few nights out at the clubs. All charged to the credit card.

Then, in a bigger move, you decide your old 1998 Saturn is on its last legs and not worthy of repair. After all, for only $259 per month, you can have a new Honda with zero-down.

The next thing you know, you've got $20,000 of consumer debt on top of a $40,000 debt for your student loans. Now, you may be paying 25% of your newly won salary to your creditors. That's after the government gets their portion. The more debt you have, the more other people own you and your productivity. It's not a very pleasant thought.

But it doesn't have to be that way. A good friend of mine once told me that if you live within your means, you will be happy no matter what your salary. Unfortunately, that's not the message society is telling you these days. It wants you to buy, consume, spend.

But there's good news. You don't have to buy into the "He who dies with the most toys wins" mentality. You don't have to have it all right away. You don't need to compete with your peers' lifestyle. You don't need to compete with your parents' lifestyle. If you follow the three simple rules recommended by most financial planners, you will have it all…eventually. They are:

1. Put 5% - 10% of your salary away for an emergency fund. Do this until you have at least $1000 saved. Make sure this money is accessible for emergencies, but not so easily accessible that you'd be tempted to tap into it to fund your next keg party.
2. If at all possible, don't use credit cards or other forms of consumer debt. It is okay to have a credit card for an emergency use, but not to supplement your salary. Credit card debt will wipe you out as quickly as a Las Vegas blackjack dealer. The odds are against you.
3. Once you've established your emergency fund, start setting aside funds for your retirement. I know it's 40 or 50 years away, but believe me, a few hundred dollars saved per month starting now could grow, with compounding, to a huge pile of dollars over time if you start early enough. For every year you delay, you will be losing tens of thousands of dollars when you're ready for retirement.

Of all the areas in your life that could now use additional research and planning, it is your personal finances and spending habits. This chapter is not enough. There are books by people like Dave Ramsey and Suze Orman that are great reads and can guide you in simple terms to a great financial future.

40

Just When You Thought it Was Safe – Continuing Education

After sixteen or more years of school, the last thing you may be thinking about is going back for more. No more teachers, no more books, no more tests and pop quizzes. If that is your attitude, I get it. I thought I would never ever open a text book again once I got my degree.

But, the funny thing is, when I looked around me, I noticed it was the life-long learners who seemed to be getting ahead. They were always challenging themselves by getting a masters degree, some type of specialized certification, or just taking courses to learn a new skill. And our employers noticed it and rewarded them for it.

The best thing about taking classes at this point is that you can do it on your terms. You can be very selective about the types of classes you want to take. You can take a class to learn a new language, a new technical skill, or to attain a certain professional certification. You can take classes on-line or in person. You can take classes at a local junior college or enroll in a formal program at a university.

With all of the options, it's never been easier to take classes. And frankly, the sooner you start taking classes, the better. If you keep putting it off, you'll have a collection of excuses for why you don't have the time, money, energy, etc. to start. Every year that passes will be that much harder to get started.

Continuing your education has many other benefits. It tells your employer you want to go farther. In fact, they may even reimburse you for your expense. Continuing your education is also a great way to enhance your resume and future job opportunities since employers are always looking for the most educated and skilled employees they can find. And, of course, continuing your education will also help you meet new people which may be important if you have moved to a new part of the country.

It used to be that very few people got a college education. Now getting a college degree is more than expected...it's a given. Although the diploma is a great accomplishment, it may not distinguish people like it once did. Now, the bar has been raised. If you want to stand out, you need to offer more to your employer. Going back to school is one of the best ways to do that.

41

On Fitness & Nutrition

Getting used to a new job also may mean getting used to a new lifestyle. Also, if you were active in athletics or had some other physical pursuits in college, you may find that it is now difficult to fit that into your new schedule. While I am not a fitness and nutrition expert, I do recognize that if you dramatically change your diet and exercise routine for the worse, you will not have that "sound mind in a sound body" perspective you need to be the best you can be at your new position.

From a nutrition standpoint, here are just a few tips to incorporate in your diet. First, stay away from living a fast-food diet. Eating burgers and fried chicken every day at lunch will zap your energy levels and will add a layer of fat around your waist quicker than you could say, "Would you like some fries with that?"

Next, try to eat high water-content, high nutrient-content whole foods. That basically means eating more fresh fruits, vegetables and whole grains. Also, try to drink plenty of fresh water throughout the business day. It will keep your body going better than will a double-shot mocha latte and will cost less, too.

Also, try to join a health club or use the fitness club in your apartment complex if one exists. Joining a club will give you access to good equipment, is a good way to pamper yourself and may be a good way to meet new people if you have moved to a new area of the country. The physical exertion will also prove to be a good stress relief and will keep you sharp.

I have said quite a few times in this book that image is extremely important to your advancement potential. A good image comes not only from external things like how you dress and the words you use, but also from within; from how you feel about yourself. A friend of mine likes to say, "If you feel good, you look good."

Eating right and maintaining a normal work-out routine will give you the foundation you need to meet the challenges of your new lifestyle.

42

Honesty is Still The Best Policy

Don't Lie. Don't Lie.

OK…so have I made my point? I could end this Quick Hit right here because I don't know how much more clearly I can make this point. Of all the things you could possibly do to torpedo your budding career, lying may be one of the worst. Lying always makes things worse. Pretty soon you don't remember what story you told whom and your credibility is shot.

Honesty should be integral to everything you do, whether it's communicating with a customer or submitting an expense report. I once worked for a small company where every penny mattered and was counted. One of the workers consistently submitted what appeared to be inflated receipts for her business meals. After receiving quite a few of these receipts, the company bookkeeper called the restaurant and asked to have several of the receipts looked up, as each receipt is numbered. When the amount the restaurant reported did not match the amount the employee submitted, she was fired.

As Mark Twain said, "Always tell the truth. That way you don't have to remember what you said." If it isn't already, make this one of your life mottos. You'll never regret telling the truth, even when it's difficult. But you will never know when a lie will turn around to bite you in your backside. And, as the previous story illustrates, even the smallest lie can cost you your job.

43

The Golden Rule

Treat others in the same way you would like to be treated. That is the sum of The Golden Rule. I've referred to principle often throughout this book. There's a good reason for that. When something is dead-on right, it bears repeating and repeating with emphasis.

Make no mistake. I'm not suggesting you ignore everything else in these pages. Among other things, we've discussed tips and techniques for improving your image, your skills, and your attitude within the company. But if you were to choose to apply only one idea from this book, the one I would recommend over all the others would be to implement The Golden Rule in your life. In your work life, your social life, and your family life. Practice it in every aspect of every thing you do.

It is always easy to be nice and respectful to people who can do something for you, but it's incredibly rewarding to be nice to someone who will never have the chance to pay you back.

I'm not a student of Eastern Religions, but I do believe in the concept of Karma. Trust that in the big scheme of things, what comes around goes around. In business terms, you will always yield a net positive return on investment when you treat others with respect, dignity and kindness.

For you, that return on investment will no doubt be a one-way ticket up the corporate ladder.

Part 5

Final Analysis

What do you want people to think about when someone mentions your name? What are the words you want to have pop into people's mind when they think of you or when you walk into the room? Are they words like reliable, trustworthy, winner, go-getter, dependable, and leader? If so, you now have everything you need to make the beginning of your career a time of excitement, growth and a whole lot of fun.

Practice what you have learned in these pages and you will no doubt be able to look back in a few years with amazement at the personal growth you've achieved. You'll be astonished by the heights you've achieved in your career, by the number of steps you've climbed on the Corporate Ladder.

It is not enough to just read these things and have head knowledge about what you need to do. You need to put them into action. Not next week. Not as a New Year's Resolution. Now is the time to act.

Start today and be consistent. You've heard it said that first impressions last. But you may also know that in the world today, many people have short memories. You have to be constant and steady. My son, who is a member of the United States Marine Corps, once told me that "the last thing you do is the first thing by which you'll be remembered." I totally agree with him.

So is it first impressions or is it the last thing you do? Yes. It's both. You have to start strong and finish stronger.

The world is hungry for hard working, ethical and principled leadership. It needs people who burn with passion for what they do. One look at the headlines and you'll know that the need is as great within the business world as it is any where else. There is a big hole, a dark void, just waiting for people like you to fill it. If you do, it will be like a vacuum pulling you up to the very top of the ladder.

That's my goal and my hope for you. To reach the top. To be the

best that you can be. To take advantage of every opportunity for
advancement that will be presented to you as you move through
your career.

I am so excited for you. I can't wait until you send out that first thank
you note to someone. I can't wait for you to iron your first shirt. I
can't wait for you to start your brag file.

Now one last thing before we part. That is to thank you for reading
this book. Thank you for making this investment in yourself and
in your future. Please keep in touch. Let me know how you do. I
would love nothing more than to get a note, an email or a letter from
you telling me about your success and how these techniques helped
you get ahead. Better yet, I would love to read about your success
in the Wall Street Journal. When the reporter asks you to what you
attribute your success, just say, "It all started with Corporate Ladder
101." I'll get the message.